Reviews of No

"SCHOLARLY, INFORMATIVE, AND BOLD. . . . Rich in insights into how gay and lesbian adolescents develop and learn to cope with problems attendant on growing up different. As a civil rights lawyer, gay rights advocate, and public servant, I am pleased by the groundbreaking work described here that has been done with child welfare departments, law enforcement, the public schools, and mental health agencies in educating them to the special needs of the gay and lesbian youngsters they inevitably will serve."
— The Honorable Roberta Achtenberg, From the Foreword

"BRILLIANT. . . . ABSOLUTELY MUST READING FOR ALL WHO VALUE THE LIVES AND FUTURES OF THE YOUNG PEOPLE IN THE LESBIAN AND GAY COMMUNITY and for all Americans who seek a truly integrated and compassionate society. . . . I commend this book to all who care."
— Marvin Liebman, Author, *Coming Out Conservative;* President, National Coalition for Understanding

"I wish this book had been available when I was growing up because it would have eased the pain and isolation I experienced growing up gay. IT SHOULD BE READ BY EVERY TEACHER, GUIDANCE COUNSELOR, SOCIAL WORKER, OR PRINCIPAL WHO WORKS WITH AMERICA'S GAY AND LESBIAN ADOLESCENTS."
—Michael Petrolis, Founder, Gay & Lesbian Americans, Washington, DC

"Goes far in correcting oversights by community agencies. . . . The carefully selected topics include developmental issues, counseling, social stigmatization, social policy, and the legal issues affecting gay and lesbian adolescents. SHOULD BE READ BY EDUCATORS, SOCIAL WORKERS, THERAPISTS, AND POLICYMAKERS CONCERNED WITH THE WELL-BEING OF OUR SOCIETY'S YOUTH."
— Richard A. Isay, MD, Clinical Professor of Psychiatry, Cornell University Medical College; Vice President, National Lesbian and Gay Health Association; Author, *Being Homosexual: Gay Men and Their Development*

Helping Gay and Lesbian Youth: New Policies, New Programs, New Practice

Helping Gay and Lesbian Youth: New Policies, New Programs, New Practice

Teresa DeCrescenzo, MSW
Editor

Helping Gay and Lesbian Youth: New Policies, New Programs, New Practice, edited by Teresa DeCrescenzo, was simultaneously issued by The Haworth Press, Inc., under the same title, as a special issue of the *Journal of Gay & Lesbian Social Services*, Volume 1, Numbers 3/4 1994, James J. Kelly, and Raymond M. Berger, Editors.

Harrington Park Press
An Imprint of
The Haworth Press, Inc.
New York · London · Norwood (Australia)

1-56023-057-6

Published by

Harrington Park Press, 10 Alice Street, Binghamton, NY 13904-1580 USA

Harrington Park Press is an imprint of The Haworth Press, Inc., 10 Alice Street, Binghamton, NY 13904-1580 USA.

Helping Gay and Lesbian Youth: New Policies, New Programs, New Practice has also been published as *Journal of Gay & Lesbian Social Services,* Volume 1, Numbers 3/4 1994.

The development, preparation, and publication of this work has been undertaken with great care. However, the publisher, employees, editors, and agents of The Haworth Press and all imprints of The Haworth Press, Inc., including The Haworth Medical Press and Pharmaceutical Products Press, are not responsible for any errors contained herein or for consequences that may ensue from use of materials or information contained in this work. Opinions expressed by the author(s) are not necessarily those of The Haworth Press, Inc.

Library of Congress Cataloging-in-Publication Data

Helping gay and lesbian youth : new policies, new programs, new practice / Teresa DeCrescenzo, editor.
     p. cm.
     "Has also been published as Journal of Gay & Lesbian Social Services, Volume 1, Numbers 3/4, 1994"–T. p. verso.
     Includes bibliographical references and index.
     ISBN 1-56024-678-2 (alk. paper). –ISBN 1-56023-057-6 (alk. paper)
     1. Gay youth–Services for–United States. 2. Gay teenagers–Services for–United States. 3. Lesbian teenagers–Services for–United States. 4. Social work with gays–United States. 5. Social work with lesbians–United States. I. DeCrescenzo, Teresa.
HV1449.H45 1994
362.7'08'664–dc20

         94-31968
         CIP

This book is lovingly dedicated

to the memory of Griffith Evan Humphreys, PhD. He was a social worker's social worker, who spoke often and eloquently about the importance of bearing witness.

and

to Betty Berzon, PhD, lover, teacher, mentor. She knows how much she contributed to this book, and I know how much better a volume it is because of her efforts.

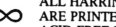

INDEXING & ABSTRACTING

Contributions to this publication are selectively indexed or abstracted in print, electronic, online, or CD-ROM version(s) of the reference tools and information services listed below. This list is current as of the copyright date of this publication. See the end of this section for additional notes.

- *AIDS Newsletter (CAB Abstracts),* CAB International, Wallingford Oxon OX10 8DE, England

- *Cambridge Scientific Abstracts, Risk Abstracts,* Cambridge Information Group, 7200 Wisconsin Avenue #601, Bethesda, MD 20814

- *caredata CD: the social and community care database,* National Institute for Social Work, 5 Tavistock Place, London WC1H 9SS, England

- *Digest of Neurology and Psychiatry,* The Institute of Living, 400 Washington Street, Hartford, CT 06106

- *Family Life Educator "Abstracts Section,"* ETR Associates, P.O. Box 1830, Santa Cruz, CA 95061-1830

- *Index to Periodical Articles Related to Law,* University of Texas, 727 East 26th Street, Austin, TX 78705

- *Inventory of Marriage and Family Literature (online and hard copy),* National Council on Family Relations, 3989 Central Avenue NE, Suite 550, Minneapolis, MN 55421

- *Referativnyi Zhurnal (Abstracts Journal of the Institute of Scientific Information of the Republic of Russia),* The Institute of Scientific Information, Baltijskaja ul., 14, Moscow A-219, Republic of Russia

(continued)

- *Social Work Abstracts,* National Association of Social Workers, 750 First Street NW, 8th Floor, Washington, DC 20002

- *Sociological Abstracts (SA),* Sociological Abstracts, Inc., P.O. Box 22206, San Diego, CA 92192-0206

- *Studies on Women Abstracts,* Carfax Publishing Company, P.O. Box 25, Abingdon, Oxfordshire OX14 3UE, United Kingdom

SPECIAL BIBLIOGRAPHIC NOTES

*related to special journal issues (separates)
and indexing/abstracting*

☐ indexing/abstracting services in this list will also cover material in the "separate" that is co-published simultaneously with Haworth's special thematic journal issue or DocuSerial. Indexing/abstracting usually covers material at the article/chapter level.

☐ monographic co-editions are intended for either non-subscribers or libraries which intend to purchase a second copy for their circulating collections.

☐ monographic co-editions are reported to all jobbers/wholesalers/approval plans. The source journal is listed as the "series" to assist the prevention of duplicate purchasing in the same manner utilized for books-in-series.

☐ to facilitate user/access services all indexing/abstracting services are encouraged to utilize the co-indexing entry note indicated at the bottom of the first page of each article/chapter/contribution.

☐ this is intended to assist a library user of any reference tool (whether print, electronic, online, or CD-ROM) to locate the monographic version if the library has purchased this version but not a subscription to the source journal.

☐ individual articles/chapters in any Haworth publication are also available through the Haworth Document Delivery Services (HDDS).

CONTENTS

ABOUT THE EDITOR

Teresa DeCrescenzo, MSW, is Founding Executive Director of Gay & Lesbian Adolescent Social Services (GLASS) in California. Among the services provided by GLASS are group homes for sexual minority youth and HIV-infected teens and a foster family agency which places children of all ages. Ms. DeCrescenzo's clinical experience includes nearly fifteen years on the staff of the Dorothy F. Kirby Center, a co-sexual residential adolescent treatment facility. After leaving Kirby Center in 1984, she designed and implemented the milieu treatment program at Arlington Group Home, a small residence providing social work and case management services to boys and girls experiencing sexual orientation conflict, or who are gay or lesbian. The success of the Arlington Group Home program led to the development of GLASS. Ms. DeCrescenzo maintains a private psychotherapy practice that includes individual, family, and group therapy, and has served as a trainer and consultant to mental health and social service agencies. A member of the National Association of Social Workers, she was named Social Worker of the Year by that organization in 1988.

Foreword

I would describe *Helping Gay and Lesbian Youth,* edited by Teresa DeCrescenzo, as scholarly, informative, and bold. There was a time, not too long ago, when social services for homosexual youth were considered too risky for gay and lesbian adult professionals to undertake. Intimidated by the possibility that their attention to these young people might be misinterpreted, activists across the nation talked about the importance of providing help for gay and lesbian teens, but capitulated to homophobia and virtually nothing was done.

As the gay and lesbian movement gained momentum and respectability, however, courageous advocates began to come forth with proposals for a wide variety of services for this underdefined and underserved population of gay youngsters. Now, at the beginning of the 1990s, determination has superseded fear, and there are a multitude of programs addressing the needs of self-identified gay and lesbian young people. That is a triumph of will, spirit, and know-how.

To understand the significance of this development one has only to think about what it is like to be a homosexual teenager as opposed to being a heterosexual teenager. Where do most adolescents go for guidance, for support, for assistance when they have a

---

The Honorable Roberta Achtenberg, JD, is the first appointed openly lesbian or gay person to be nominated by any President and confirmed by the United States Senate. She is the former Executive Director of the National Center for Lesbian Rights in San Francisco, and a former elected member of the San Francisco County Board of Supervisors.

[Haworth co-indexing entry note]: "Foreword." Achtenberg, Roberta. Co-published simultaneously in *Journal of Gay & Lesbian Social Services* (The Haworth Press, Inc.) Vol. 1, No. 3/4, 1994, pp. xv-xviii: and: *Helping Gay and Lesbian Youth: New Policies, New Programs, New Practice* (ed: Teresa DeCrescenzo) The Haworth Press, Inc., 1994, pp. xiii-xvi. Multiple copies of this article/chapter may be purchased from The Haworth Document Delivery Center [1-800-3-HAWORTH; 9:00 a.m. - 5:00 p.m. (EST)].

problem? To their own families, of course. But, for gay and lesbian teenagers, the *last* place they are likely to go is the family, because it is the family finding out about their sexual orientation that they are usually most afraid of.

The need for some adult, agency, or organization to stand, temporarily, in *loco parentis* is essential to the mental health, and sometimes to the survival, of many gay or lesbian teenagers. The essays in this volume describe the impressive array of programs now available to do just that.

But that is just part of the story. This collection is rich in insights into how gay and lesbian adolescents develop and learn to cope with the problems attendant on growing up different. As a civil rights lawyer, gay rights advocate, and public servant, I am pleased by the groundbreaking work described here that has been done with child welfare departments, law enforcement, the public schools, and mental health agencies in educating them to the special needs of the gay and lesbian youngsters they inevitably will serve.

As a parent, it is almost incomprehensible to me that there are mothers and fathers of gay and lesbian teenagers who push their kids out the door on learning that they are gay. Incomprehensible, but true. From all over the United States these pushed out kids come to the large cities, New York, Los Angeles, Boston, Chicago, Washington, D.C., San Francisco, to find the underground groups of youngsters like themselves to throw in with, to learn from how to live on the streets. They do learn and the lessons are often brutal and dehumanizing. They end up prostituting and dealing drugs, a life that, one would think, no parent could possibly wish on their offspring.

Fortunately, organizations exist that are prepared to intervene, organizations like Gay and Lesbian Adolescent Social Services (GLASS) in Los Angeles which provides group and foster homes for sexual minority youth, the Gay and Lesbian Community Services Center of Los Angeles (GLCSC) which operates transitional housing for homeless gay and lesbian youth, Horizons in Chicago, the Sexual Minority Assistance League (SMYAL) in Washington, D.C., the Boston Alliance of Gay and Lesbian Youth (BAGLY) in Boston, and the Hetrick-Martin Institute in New York. The homeless gay or lesbian teenager need no longer be alone, or dependent on the streets for survival.

Abby Abinati's article in this book on *Legal Challenges Facing Lesbian and Gay Youth* brings together in one place issues regarding gay and nongay guardianship, adoption, emancipation from parental custody and control, and due process in school matters. It also explains the workings of the child welfare and juvenile court systems.

Anyone involved in the care or treatment of sexual minority youngsters would do well to be familiar with the issues presented in Abinati's essay. Because there are so many gay and lesbian youth in "chosen family constellations," the issues of guardianship and emancipation are important to understand. Due process in school matters speaks to the refusal of gay and lesbian people to continue to be passive victims of other people's prejudices. And, knowing one's way around the child welfare and juvenile court systems can help a youngster to make the best use of the legal and social service options available.

Of course, many gay and lesbian teenagers are not banished from their homes and do enjoy the support of their families. We have made that much progress in educating the American public to the truth of what it means to be gay. The challenge involving these youngsters is to educate the educators so that school social environments and school curricula reflect the existence and acceptability of students who happen to be gay or lesbian.

Nancy Taylor's article here on social policy refers to homophobic faculty and administrations in some schools who have either condoned or perpetrated discriminatory acts against gay or lesbian students. Such behavior has prompted the formation of several separate junior high and high schools that enroll only gay and lesbian students, in order to provide safe and affirming environments for learning. Notable are the EAGLES Center in Los Angeles and the Harvey Milk School in New York City.

In a particularly innovative move, the state of Massachusetts has initiated training seminars on the unique needs of gay and lesbian youth for teachers and school-district representatives. Massachusetts Governor William Weld says of this program, "We can take the first step toward ending gay youth suicide by creating an atmosphere of dignity and respect for gay youth in our schools."

"Project 10," the program launched in 1984 at Los Angeles's Fairfax High School by teacher Virginia Uribe, is another example of breaking through public school conservatism to create a safe haven for sexual minority youth. Project 10 provides counseling and support for gay and lesbian students and serves as a model for similar programs starting up across the country.

So, little by little, we are fulfilling our responsibility to the young people for whom we do stand in *loco parentis* in a variety of ways. This collection of essays strengthens our stand with its comprehensive overview of the research on gay youth, its state of the art commentary on treatment and prevention issues, and its thought-provoking chapters on social policy and gay and lesbian youth advocacy. The editor and the authors deserve bouquets for their efforts.

Roberta Achtenberg, JD

Preface

Where the needs of gay and lesbian adolescents are at stake, the Federal government has the most ground to make up, since it has the money, influence, and access to establish an enlightened approach to serving the unmet needs of this population. Most of what is done in Federal government is potentially about politics. Apparently, the politics of prejudice are as malignant in the Washington corridors of power as they are in Bible-belt America.

Politics drives policy in Washington. Just as the gays in the military issue became, more than anything, a political football, any attempt aimed at funding, developing, and utilizing research on the lives of gay and lesbian youngsters would likely suffer a similar fate. Only if efforts in this area are kept out of the hands of politicians as much as possible, can assessment of problems and implementation of programs for these youngsters ever happen on the scale it deserves. One wonders what people are so afraid of? Why can't Federal agencies pay more attention to this minority population who have so many obstacles to overcome just in the process of growing up? What is the threat that homosexuality holds for so many, and, unfortunately, for so many in positions of power? Some would say it's about their religious beliefs. Though religion ought never to be about condemning, excluding, and punishing innocent people, it sometimes apparently is. It is incumbent upon us not to accept that particular tradition as a rationale for a government reneging on its responsibility to serve the needs of the people, in this instance the needs of young people.

For some, antipathy toward gays is about their own discomfort

[Haworth co-indexing entry note]: "Preface." DeCrescenzo, Teresa. Co-published simultaneously in *Journal of Gay & Lesbian Social Services* (The Haworth Press, Inc.) Vol. 1, No. 3/4, 1994, pp. *xix-xxiv*: and: *Helping Gay and Lesbian Youth: New Policies, New Programs, New Practice* (ed: Teresa DeCrescenzo) The Haworth Press, Inc., 1994, pp. *xvii-xxii*. Multiple copies of this article/chapter may be purchased from The Haworth Document Delivery Center [1-800-3-HAWORTH; 9:00 a.m. - 5:00 p.m. (EST)].

with sexuality–theirs and everybody else's. They believe the false stereotype that gays are all about sex. For others it is their family legacy. They learned growing up to fear homosexuality and to hate gay and lesbian people. There are also those individuals who resist change of any kind, and the increasing visibility and social acceptance of open gays and lesbians challenge the security they feel from the old and the familiar.

Mostly, however, the threat of gays and lesbians is about the force of bigotry. Bigotry has its own rewards. People who depend on hating and excluding others to achieve self-validation for themselves can be understood in the context of their own lives. Boredom, powerlessness, and anger are at the heart of their behavior. The choice of a targeted group to discriminate against is usually influenced by those who have a lot to gain from mobilizing people into a constituency willing to give the time, energy, and money that add up to political power. These are the people who write to the White House, call the Congress, and lobby to thwart any social change that would offer groups such as needy gay and lesbian teenagers the slightest help for their lives.

What is most reprehensible about this, is the capitulation of politicians to the factions of bigotry when it comes to assistance that would benefit anyone gay or lesbian, even teenagers in need. It is supposed to be everybody's government, but a look at the funding record of research and demonstration projects that the Federal government supports says otherwise. Noticeably missing are funded studies designed to learn more about, and improve, the lives of the gay and lesbian citizens of this country.

It is particularly deplorable when it is adolescents who are being short-changed. For instance, we suspect that gay and lesbian teenagers who have internalized society's rejection of them, may commit suicide in greater numbers than their heterosexual counterparts. Without large-scale studies on this subject we don't know how many gay adolescents take their own lives. A nationally conducted, Federally funded study could begin to answer this critically important question.

The world of any adolescent is complicated. There are sexual issues, identity issues, confusing physiological growth and development, the temptations of alcohol and drugs, and parental conflicts.

Added to this are the issues of sexual identity, of feeling different, less than, terribly flawed, an outcast. This is what most gay or lesbian youth face. Some work it through. Some do not. Some find solace in social service programs of the gay and lesbian community. Some choose isolation and self-hate. The more resilient ones make it into adulthood relatively unscathed. Others make it into adulthood emotionally scarred. Some don't make it into adulthood at all.

What a difference it would make if there were more supportive and validating programs for gay and lesbian adolescents to avail themselves of, in the schools, in the community, in religious settings. How much it would help to know that you are a normal, natural person, as good as anyone else, that you don't have to be ashamed of who you are, or afraid to tell anyone about it. What wasted lives could be saved. What wasted talents could be put to work. What productive energies could be preserved. What love could be freed up to make the world a gentler, safer place.

In order to make this happen, there are moral, social, and political minefields to be traversed. Is the present administration ready to take on this challenge, to stare down the forces of bigotry, to put the needs of homosexual youngsters before the needs of individuals who must oppose and spoil and denigrate good works that do not benefit them, or those just like them?

The current administration has taken several giant steps forward, and several giant steps backward in this matter. The silence is once and for all broken about gays in America. But the silence has been replaced by a powerful homophobic backlash, including the perpetuation of damaging false stereotypes by some of the highest officials in our government. Is this the administration that will lead in terms of the needs of its gay and lesbian citizens, that will support and defend programs to give homosexual teenagers the opportunities for self-validation and personal growth that their heterosexual counterparts take for granted? It seems not.

Until that leadership exists at the Federal level, we must look to AIDS activists for the model of empowerment and action. We must be prepared to do it for ourselves. The gay and lesbian community has performed a series of miracles in caregiving, in fund-raising, and in public education regarding AIDS. Some have complained in the past that there has been a lack of role models in the gay world.

One has only to look to the heroes of AIDS care to find the courage, determination, stamina, intelligence, and compassion almost beyond belief, to emulate.

Gay and lesbian adults in the arts, sciences, and professions are coming out in larger numbers than ever before, thus the gay or lesbian teenager can see what the possibilities are for being gay and successful. Books are being written by and for gay youth that can break through the isolation of the worried youngster with no one to talk to, no one with whom to identify. Youth groups are forming in gay centers all over the country, giving youth a safe place to go, contacts to make that also dispel isolation.

Where is the Federal government in all this, to help the grassroot groups put on their programs, and, perhaps more importantly, to expand and fund public education about homosexuality, so that ordinary, good, decent citizens who have never had a reason to question their anti-gay prejudices will have reason to begin to do so?

Where are the school systems, responsible to all their students, willing to present curricula that include gay and lesbian issues, willing to present the reality of cultural diversity to their students? Where are the Federal grants to support such programs?

The present administration appears more willing than previous administrations to deal with such issues as health care reform, individual rights, and the social consciousness of young people. But we have heard nothing about any of those things as they involve gay and lesbian teenagers. Could it be that the legislators and bureaucrats believe that gay teenagers don't exist? It seems unlikely, since there are those among them who have children or other relatives who are gay or lesbian. Unfortunately, most politicians appear to possess extraordinary ability to stare an issue right in the face and claim that it doesn't really exist. That is what happened with gays in the military, and it appears to be what is happening with governmental acknowledgement of the needs of gay and lesbian youth.

How could acknowledgment of gay and lesbian youth occur? What would it translate to? For instance, such acknowledgement could be included in the grant award criteria of Federal agencies funding research and demonstration projects on teenage alcohol and drug abuse, homelessness, and other high risk activities. Instead, when the organizations that provide services to the gay and lesbian population apply for grants, they must often disguise their real mission with euphemisms that exclude or downplay the words "gay and lesbian."

What an important message would be sent to the millions of gay kids, their families, their teachers, and their peers to have the affirming support of the Federal government in their effort to become good gay and lesbian citizens. What a tribute to the reality-testing powers of government officials to publicly recognize that there really are young people who know they are homosexual, and are willing to identify as such. The domino effect of such validation would positively impact millions of Americans who are, are related to, or just know someone who is gay or lesbian.

Because there is not the kind of Federal support discussed here, research conducted to date on such things as sexual orientation as a risk factor in suicide attempts among youth has not been comprehensive, and cannot accurately provide generalizable conclusions. Clearly, such a comprehensive study is urgently needed.

The dollars that have been forthcoming from Federal funding agencies have mostly been targeted for high risk gay youth. Important as that is, often even a matter of survival for these kids, there is another population that also needs the attention of researchers. The middle-class gay or lesbian adolescent who is struggling with identity issues, sexual conflicts, fear of parental rejection and the judgment of peers, has been virtually ignored by researchers, social workers, and other service providers. Their struggle can become life-threatening, or it can be the foundation for an extremely productive adult life. Why are some of these youngsters so resilient, not only surviving, but also thriving? What causes others to become too damaged to cope successfully with life? We need studies to answer these questions, and we need significant policy changes at the highest levels of government. Change is in the air.

Consider Nancy Taylor's thoughtful, informed paper on social policy issues. It is a blueprint for change, as is Abby Abinati's contribution to this volume. Both papers are thorough, persuasive, and challenging.

Dennis Durby's comprehensive paper on the "status" of gay and lesbian youth in this country is neither overly optimistic, nor excessively pessimistic. It does, however, clearly illustrate the dearth of methodologically sound, replicable research available about this population, particularly in the area of suicide.

Sullivan and Jackson argue persuasively for the need to examine our own perspectives, and the implications for ethical practice grounded in advocacy, while Mallon offers specific counseling strategies to employ with gay and lesbian youth.

Finally, homophobia is addressed in every paper, whether as an obstacle to full development, as a factor in social policies, as an impediment to achieving full legal status, whether personal or institutionalized. It informs the actions and reactions of the policy makers, legislators, religious practitioners, and service providers in this country. Each paper in this volume challenges the reader.

Who, then, is in the best position to make these challenges to the Federal government of the United States? Is it the grassroots gay and lesbian groups fighting for equality and justice in their lives? Is it the direct action groups turning up the volume on issues that affect all gay and lesbian people, even those who disagree with their methods?

Is it the suited-up establishment activists who work from the inside to change the social climate for gays? Is it the few openly gay or lesbian individuals in positions of power–elected officials, coaxed-out movie moguls, wealthy benefactors, influential intellectuals? Is it the ordinary gay or lesbian person who goes into the voting booth fully informed about the candidates who are most likely to deliver for gay and lesbian civil rights? Is it the enlightened nongay politicos and professionals who have the wisdom to understand that what happens to the gay and lesbian people in this country happens to every person who cherishes citizenship in a democracy?

The challenge, of course, must be met by all of the above, and by you, and me, and by everyone who cares about the well-being of young people, including those who happen to be gay or lesbian.

Teresa DeCrescenzo, MSW

Acknowledgments

I would like to thank Abby Abinati, Dennis Durby, Greg Greeley, Darryl Jackson, Gerald Mallon, Bill Pederson, Richard Sullivan, and Nancy Taylor for their contributions to the growing body of literature on the special needs of sexual minority youth. These papers represent thoughtful, informed offerings, which will both enlighten and challenge the reader.

Special thanks are also due Lorraine Beltran, who was always willing to make "just one more" change in the manuscript. My gratitude also goes to Margaret Jacoby, my executive assistant, whose organizational skills kept this project moving in the midst of other projects competing for my attention.

Dr. Raymond M. Berger demonstrated uncommon patience, offered his support and encouragement generously, and did a lot of "therapeutic holding" throughout this project, for which I am most appreciative.

I am genuinely thankful to the Honorable Roberta Achtenberg, for taking the time to review and comment on this lengthy manuscript.

As always, I must give credit to my life partner of the past twenty-one years, Dr. Betty Berzon, who is consistently willing to take time from her own writing to read a paper, and offer gentle criticisms and suggestions.

Finally, I would like to recognize and honor the millions of gay and lesbian youth who have been living lives of courage, without enough guidance from those of us who have been there. This book is for you.

[Haworth co-indexing entry note]: "Acknowledgments." Co-published simultaneously in *Journal of Gay & Lesbian Social Services* (The Haworth Press, Inc.) Vol. 1, No. 3/4, 1994, p. *xxv*: and: *Helping Gay and Lesbian Youth: New Policies, New Programs, New Practice* (ed: Teresa DeCrescenzo) The Haworth Press, Inc., 1994, p. *xxiii*. Multiple copies of this article/chapter may be purchased from The Haworth Document Delivery Center [1-800-3-HAWORTH; 9:00 a.m. - 5:00 p.m. (EST)].

Gay, Lesbian, and Bisexual Youth

Dennis D. Durby

SUMMARY. Adolescence is a period fraught with developmental challenges for all individuals. Those encountered by gay, lesbian, bisexual, and other sexual minority[1] youth are particularly difficult. The knowledge that they are "different" somehow, although not yet necessarily fully aware of how they are different, leaves many isolated and unable to work through some typical developmental issues having to do with establishing romantic relationships and learning diverse social skills. Such teens may develop a host of coping mechanisms to ease the dissonance experienced when their forming identities are in conflict with peer, parental or, more broadly, societal expectations.

Lesbian, gay, and bisexual youth comprise an unknown, but significant, percentage of young persons.

Writing for The Respect All Youth Project of the Federation of Parents and Friends of Lesbians and Gays, Cook and Pawlowski (1991) offer the following: Some youth are lesbian or gay. Some

---

Dennis D. Durby, MSW, is a clinical social worker and administrative program consultant in West Hollywood, CA. He is completing his PhD in Social Work at the University of Southern California School of Social Work, where he has been a Pre-Doctoral Merit Fellow.

The author wishes to thank Teresa DeCrescenzo, MSW, for her encouragement and contributions to the completion of this paper.

Correspondence may be directed to the author at 650 N. Robertson Blvd., Suite A, West Hollywood, CA 90069.

[Haworth co-indexing entry note]: "Gay, Lesbian, and Bisexual Youth." Durby, Dennis D. Co-published simultaneously in *Journal of Gay & Lesbian Social Services* (The Haworth Press, Inc.) Vol. 1, No. 3/4, 1994, pp. 1-37; and: *Helping Gay and Lesbian Youth: New Policies, New Programs, New Practice* (ed: Teresa DeCrescenzo) The Haworth Press, Inc., 1994, pp. 1-37. Multiple copies of this article/chapter may be purchased from The Haworth Document Delivery Center [1-800-3-HAWORTH; 9:00 a.m. - 5:00 p.m. (EST)].

1

youth are labeled lesbian or gay by others, whether they are or not. Some youth have lesbian or gay parents, siblings, or other relatives. These young people all suffer because of the stigma and prejudices surrounding homosexuality. Even more young people—including heterosexual youth—make important life decisions based on stigma, prejudice, and rampant misinformation, rather than on what is healthy and right for them (p. 1).

BACKGROUND

Lesbian, gay, and bisexual youth are an invisible, mostly ignored, segment of American society. They are forgotten both because of their invisibility, and because of the stigma inherent in the identification of persons as gay or lesbian or bisexual. Hammersmith (1987, p. 176) notes that this stigma "threatens both self-esteem and one's sense of identity by denying the social and emotional validation upon which those constructs are built." Youth are generally presumed to have a heterosexual orientation, and contemporary social institutions from families to schools are grounded in this notion. Savin-Williams suggests:

> Most youth are raised in heterosexual families, associate in heterosexual peer groups, and are educated in heterosexual institutions. Youth who are not heterosexual often feel they have little option except to pass as "heterosexually normal." The fact that they must hide their sexual orientation makes it assume a global significance to them considerably beyond necessary proportions. (1990, p. 1)

Thus, during the period of adolescence, the difficulties involved in completing developmental tasks are compounded by the young person's attention to concealing her or his sexual feelings and identity, to the conflicts around the expression of those feelings, and to coping with issues of self-image and self-esteem.

Invisibility often extends to gay, lesbian, and bisexual youth themselves. Anecdotal reports of many lesbians and gay men reveal that there are many roads to the self-discovery that one is lesbian or gay (or bisexual). This process may span years, beginning in childhood and extending into adulthood. Malyon (1982) posits a biphasic developmental cycle for gay males in which the process of adolescent identity development is interrupted by the phenomenon of "homophobia."[2]

Stereotypes of homosexuals are pervasive throughout American culture, and these are largely negative. Mainstream institutions, such as churches, the legal system, the press and entertainment industries, and "traditional" values, tend to reinforce false negative stereotypes. These stereotypes have a significant impact upon the personal and social environments of youth, and tend to be reinforcing of negative attitudes in families and classmates or other peer groups.

Non-validation of homosexual orientations extends sufficiently far that the lesbian or gay adolescent may simply be seen as going through some developmental stage on the way to "healthy" heterosexual adjustment. While there is evidence that many youth, perhaps a majority, experiment with same-sex activity, for gay, lesbian, and bisexual youth this activity is primary to their orientation as persons. Parents or other adults who become aware of such activity may tend to excuse it as a developmental issue, certain that the youth will outgrow it. Others, in anger or disgust, may push out or throw away their child, leaving her/him to fend alone. Throwaway lesbians, bisexuals, and gays are found in large numbers among youth living on the streets in metropolitan areas. Such youth are ripe for exploitation by others as they strive to survive. Street life and survival may include the development of addictions to drugs, survival prostitution, exposure to the human immunodeficiency virus (HIV) and other infections, homelessness, and criminal activity.

Blake is a typical example of such a youth. Twenty-two-years-old, he was pushed out of his home in suburban Southern California at age 16, because his father found a gay-oriented magazine in his room. His parents were divorced, and he moved to California to live with his father after being raised by his mother in Ohio and New Hampshire, following her second marriage:

> I came to Hollywood to explore my sexuality after my dad threw me out. I was confused—still am—about whether I was gay or straight. Maybe I'm bisexual. I feel more intimate and close to guys, but I like being with girls too. And it makes it

easier with my family when they see me with a girl. I had tried pot before coming to L.A., and alcohol, but not much else I guess. I started hustling to see what sex was about and to get money for a room. I've done about everything. I've been heavily into crack for several years now. I've had about eight arrests for grand theft auto 'cause I would get guys I was with to give me their keys so I could go get more crack for us both, then I'd take off and get some, keep the rest of the money, and the car. No convictions though. I've been convicted of crack possession for sale, but got probation. I've done photography, and legitimate modeling–clothes and catalogs–and I have a trade in construction, but the drugs and my feelings about my sexuality have kept me feeling bad about myself. If my family had been different about it I think I wouldn't have gone through all the bad things I've gone through. I feel like my resources are expended, gone. I'm still confused about my sexuality, and guilty. I wish my family were different about it. Accepting and approving. I desperately want to get off drugs, get my life on track. I think I'm pretty bright, I know I'm good looking, and I want a real life someplace. I think I could make a difference in the world, but not like this.

It may seem to adolescents or young adults to be in their best interest to conceal their own suspicions or knowledge of their sexual orientation. Sometimes this is readily done. At other times, particularly when there is suspicion of "difference" by peers, youth may be subject to name-calling (fag, dyke, queer, homo, lesbo, and others) and sexual taunting. These experiences leave deep wounds. The youth experiences humiliation as a result of the taunts, and conflict insofar as they suspect or know that the jeers are true. The lesbian, gay, and bisexual youth who are not so teased nonetheless witness the behavior and share the pain.

Invisibility is not only reinforced, but sought. Adolescence is a particularly difficult time for self-affirmation. Affirmation of a positive sexual identity may be the most difficult developmental challenge faced by lesbian and gay youth. Conflicts around sexual identity consume vast amounts of the lesbian or gay adolescent's time and resources. School, family, and broader social activities are all impacted by these conflicts. Youth are typically encouraged or forced, at differing ages, to begin socializing individually with persons of the other gender. For the homosexual or bisexual young woman or man, this may be a particularly troubling time. Increasingly aware of attractions to persons of the same gender, the understanding of familial and societal demands forms a framework for internal conflict. At the very time when lesbian, gay, or bisexual youth would benefit from exploring same-sex social relationships, they are instead forced to deny (outwardly, at a minimum) these feelings, either substituting heterosexually-oriented social behaviors or withdrawing from all such contact. This complex of coping strategies may, in some individuals, postpone the completion of some developmental tasks until sometime in the twenties or even later.

Several theoretical models of the development of homosexual identities have been discussed by researchers over the past 15 or so years (Cass, 1979, 1984; Coleman, 1982; Lee, 1977; Malyon, 1982; Ponse, 1978; Schäfer, 1976; Troiden, 1979; 1984/1985; 1988; 1989; Troiden & Goode, 1980). Troiden offers a four-stage theoretical model to describe the development of homosexual identity: sensitization, identity confusion, identity assumption, and commitment.

In the *sensitization* stage, which is prepubertal, the young person experiences generalized feelings of both marginalization and "differentness" from same-gender peers. Martin (1982) notes that gay and lesbian youth are often subjected to verbal abuse, physical cruelty, condemnation by organized religion, overt discrimination, or outright rejection in response to suspicion or disclosure of their homosexuality. Examples of these experiences for gay men and lesbians are cited by Bell, Weinberg, and Hammersmith (1981):

Men: I had a keener interest in the arts; I never learned to fight; I just didn't feel I was like other boys. I was very fond of pretty things like ribbons and flowers and music; I was indifferent to boy's games, like cops and robbers. I was more interested in watching insects and reflecting on certain things; I began to get feelings I was gay. (pp. 74, 86)

Women: I was very shy and unaggressive; I felt different: unfemi-
nine, ungraceful, not very pretty, kind of a mess; I was
more masculine, more independent, more aggressive,
more outdoorish; I didn't express myself the way other
girls would. For example, I never showed my feelings. I
wasn't emotional. (pp. 148, 156)

In this study, only a few of the participants reported feeling different
due to *sexual* attractions or activity. Generally, such individuals do
not report wondering at this stage whether they were homosexual,
nor do they consider that homosexuality is an issue affecting them
at all. Such childhood experiences take on meaning in terms of
personal identity at a later time, as they are associated with homosexual feeling and attractions in adolescence or beyond. "This rein-
terpretation of past events as indicating a homosexual potential
appears to be a necessary (but not sufficient) condition for the
eventual adoption of homosexual identities" (Troiden, 1989, p. 52).

The second stage Troiden posits is *identity confusion*. In this
developmental stage, lesbians and gay males, and possibly bisexuals as well, develop an awareness that their feelings and behaviors
may be related to homosexuality. Such thoughts are incongruent
with earlier self-images, according to Troiden. This results in an
internal conflict over the youth's identity, accompanied by apprehension, agitation, and questioning of his or her sexuality. Research
has suggested that the self perception that one is homosexual begins
to emerge in girls at about age 18 (Schäfer, 1976), and in boys at
about age 17 (Troiden, 1979; Troiden & Goode, 1980). Troiden
(1989, p. 53) considers several factors influencing this identity
confusion. First, altered perceptions of one's self; second, sexual
arousal and sexual behavior, whether homo- or heterosexual in
nature; third, the stigma associated with homosexuality; fourth,
insufficient information and misinformation about homosexuals
and homosexuality. Youth in this phase of development may have a
tendency to engage in solitary activities, avoiding others to avert
questions or interest about them. Or, they may avoid suspicion by
dating members of the other sex, or putting their energies into other
pursuits. Some youth may cope with this stage, and with the perceived and experienced stigma associated with homosexuality, by

running away to metropolitan areas, where they are at high risk for exploitation.

Several investigators and theorists have suggested that lesbians and gay males cope with this identity confusion in particular ways. These mechanisms include *repair* (Humphreys, 1972), *avoidance* (Cass, 1979), *redefinition* (Cass, 1979), *denial* (Goode, 1984), and *acceptance* (Cass, 1979). In *repair*, efforts are directed towards eliminating homosexual feelings or behaviors, sometimes through seeking professional assistance (therapy).

In *avoidance*, Troiden (1989) suggests that homosexual behavior, thoughts, and feelings are unacceptable to the individual, who may employ any of several strategies to cope with their status. First, they may seek to inhibit their interests. Second, they may seek to limit exposure to members of the opposite gender in an effort to prevent family or friends from discerning their lack of interest. Third, they may avoid information about sexuality or homosexuality. Fourth, they may assume staunch heterosexual social postures. If the latter is unconscious, this stratagem may represent a reaction formation, wherein they may attack and ridicule other homosexuals. Fifth, they may engage in intense heterosexual relationships, "at varying levels of intimacy in order to eliminate their 'inappropriate' sexual interests" (p. 57). Sixth, they may escape through the use of drugs, which allows both a transient assuagement of conflicting feelings and a justification for otherwise unacceptable behavior.

Redefinition involves redefining behaviors, thoughts, or feelings in a new context. Cass (1979) posits four strategies: special case, ambisexual (i.e., bisexual), temporary identity, and situational. In the instance of the special case, behavior and feelings are contextualized as isolated incidents or circumstances, never to be repeated, or at least not with anyone else. Adopting a bisexual identity for a time represents the temporary identity strategy. In this case, the individual defines her or himself as bisexual or ambisexual. Of course, some youth and adults are bisexual, and in such individuals this may be both a strategy and accurate. The temporary identity strategy involves the contextualization of homosexual thoughts, feelings, and behaviors as part of the development of the individual, a phase that will pass with time. The final redefinitional strategy is the situational, wherein the individual defines particular circumstances as responsible for homosexual fantasies or behaviors (for example, "I was really drunk last Saturday night!").

The fourth mechanism for coping with identity confusion is that of denial. In utilizing this mechanism, youth (or adults) simply deny any association between their thoughts, feelings, or behavior and homosexuality *per se*.

The final strategy, asserts Cass (1979), is that of acceptance. Persons able to accept their sexual orientation are able to resolve many of the conflicts they had been experiencing. They seek out more information and self-understanding about their thoughts and feelings, and may experience relief at finally gaining an understanding about who they are.

Troiden notes:

> Perceptions of self anchored in the strategies of denial, repair, avoidance, or redefinition may be sustained for months, years, or permanently. Bisexual (ambisexual) perceptions of self, for example, a redefinitional strategy, may be maintained or undermined by a person's social roles, position in the social structure, intimate relationships, and by the perceived strength, persistence, and salience of the homosexual feelings. Although individuals may use several different stigma-management strategies, they characteristically use some more than others. (1989, p. 58)

The third stage in Troiden's model is that of *identity assumption,* which occurs following the resolution, or partial resolution, of identity confusion. "In this stage, the homosexual identity becomes both a self-identity and a presented identity, at least to other homosexuals" (Troiden, 1989, p. 59). Self-identification and disclosure to others of the individual's homosexuality first occur here, with this information often being shared first with others who are identified as gay or lesbian themselves. This may be the first evidence of the process of coming out (Coleman, 1982). In addition to self-identification and disclosure, this developmental stage is characterized by fuller acceptance of the self, sexual exploration and sexual activity, the development of a social support network of lesbians and gay men, involvement in gay and lesbian subcultures, and exploration of different kinds of friendships and other relationships.

There may be some distancing from former (heterosexual) friends and social circles as well, as this unfolding identity may still be concealed from non-gay/non-lesbian others so as not to invite disapproval or disdain.

The age at which self-identification transpires seems to differ between young women and young men. Several retrospective studies of adult gay men (Dank, 1971; Harry & DeVall, 1978; Kooden, Morin, Riddle, Rogers et al., 1979; McDonald, 1982; Troiden, 1979) suggest that gay men generally self-identify somewhere between the ages of 19-21. A more recent retrospective study of 29 male teenagers (79% self-described as gay, 21% as bisexual) by Remafedi (1987) found that the mean age for self-identification as gay was 14 years, with 8 subjects (31%) recalling attractions to men during childhood. "As reflected in one subject's response, these memories are often vague and impressionistic" (p. 328). One such memory included:

> My first memory of being attracted to men was a dream I had when I was 6 or 7. I was in a bathtub with a man in the middle of the forest. I remember this was a happy dream for me, and I dreamt it over and over again for years. (p. 328)

Research among lesbians indicates that the assumption of a lesbian identity occurs somewhat later for women, generally from age 21-23 (Califia, 1979; Riddle & Morin, 1977; Schäfer, 1976).

Research among gay males has shown that they are less likely than lesbians to self-identify out of the context of same-sex intimate relationships. Studies by Cronin (1974) and Schäfer (1976) indicate that women are likely to self-identify while in intimate love relationships with other women. In Cronin's study of lesbians, 76% of the women studied reported that they were involved in significant and intense relationships with other women at the time of self-identification. Conversely, studies of gay males (Dank, 1971; McDonald, 1982; Troiden, 1979) revealed that only about 20% of men were in such a context at the time of their self-identification. Generally, gay men tended to self-identify in subcultural social contexts centered on sexual activities: men's rooms, public parks and rest rooms, YMCAs, gay bars, and gay social events (Dank, 1971; Troiden, 1979; Warren, 1974).

While self-identification occurs at this stage, full self-acceptance does not seem to. Cass (1979) suggests that the character of an individual's early contacts with other lesbians or gay men is critical to further development and maturation as a person. Negative initial contacts may result in a return to the behaviors and experiences of the second stage of identity confusion, with its resultant negative effects on self-esteem. The impact of this cannot be overstated. Whether one has returned to Stage 2 or never moved out of it in terms of identity confusion, the potential impact of the coping strategies which typify it are generally destructive. For example, the effects of extreme anti-homosexual attitudes of some gay individuals have entered into popular culture, as in the 1993 Pulitzer-prize-winning play *Angels in America: Millennium Approaches* by Tony Kushner. In this play, an aging Roy Cohn is portrayed as a powerful, extremely anti-gay, homosexual, who is in abject denial, at least to others, as to his homosexuality.

Conversely, this third stage seems to be successfully negotiated when positive contacts and experiences with other gay or lesbian individuals occur. Such contacts provide validation, encouragement of further growth, and positive experiences of the subculture, leading to a lessened sense of isolation and disaffection. These contacts provide opportunities for deepened reflections on these young persons' notions about themselves, their sexuality and their place in the world. They also provide enhanced opportunities for social involvements, discussions about lesbian and gay life, and role models who demonstrate self-acceptance and positive values about themselves and others.

Humphreys (1972) discusses various strategies for evading the stigma attached to homosexuality which Troiden (1989, pp. 61-62) suggests are employed in this stage: capitulation, minstrelization, passing, and group alignment.

Capitulation involves the avoidance of homosexual activities by individuals with continuing homosexual feelings and attractions, which is thought to result in self-loathing and despair. *Minstrelization* is the exhibition of sexual orientation congruent with popular stereotypes, often in "gender-inappropriate" ways. *Passing* as non-gay is the third, and possibly the most frequent, method of handling the stigma attached to being lesbian or gay. "Passers lead 'double lives,' that is, they segregate their social worlds into heterosexual and homosexual spheres and hope the two never collide" (Troiden, p. 62). Novice gays and lesbians also employ the strategy of *group alignment*, in which mode they become active participants in affirming organizations or groups in the lesbian and gay communities. Such affiliations engender a sense of membership in a broad subculture, with its attendant supports and challenges.

The fourth stage in development of a homosexual identity in Troiden's model is that of *commitment*. "In the homosexual context, *commitment* involves adopting homosexuality as a way of life." This developmental stage is characterized by an acceptance of self and a serenity towards one's status and life. The lesbian or gay youth in this stage enjoys contentment with the self as a lesbian or gay individual. Troiden (1989) posits both internal and external dimensions of commitment. In the internal dimension, sexuality and emotionality are integrated, a positive shift occurs in the individual's conceptualization of a lesbian or gay identity, and satisfaction with the self as a gay male or lesbian ensues, leading to increased happiness with one's self.

External significators of commitment include the development of same-sex romantic love relationships, which demonstrate the integration of emotionality and sexuality in the person. Women, who tend to self-identify when they are in their early twenties, seem to enter such relationships sooner after coming out (between age 21 and age 24) than do gay men, who tend to identify in their middle or late teens. Gay men seem to enter into such relationships at about the same age as women, but some two to five years after coming out.

Another means of externalizing commitment is disclosure of sexual orientation to an ever broadening audience, moving from self to other lesbians or gays to other friends, to family, employers, and so on. In the commitment stage, individuals employ different coping strategies to manage stigma from those used in earlier developmental phases. In discussing the third external index of commitment, Troiden (1989) argues that passing and group alignment are replaced by what Humphreys (1972) termed covering and blending. Those who *cover* "manage their homosexuality in ways meant to demonstrate that although they may be homosexual, they are nonetheless respectable." Those who *blend* "act in gender-appropriate ways and neither announce nor deny their homosexual identities to nonhomosexual others" (Troiden, 1989, pp. 66-67). These individuals view their orientation as irrelevant to other areas of their lives outside of the homosexual community, and keep silent. Finally, either strategy may be replaced by *conversion,* in which the lesbian or gay male adopts the perspective that both destigmatizes homosexuality and converts it to an asset or strength.

These diverse strategies are somewhat fluid. A gay male or lesbian may move among and between them throughout life's stages, depending upon circumstance and attitude. Importantly for lesbian and gay youth, the emergence of identity is a process rather than an event. As process, it is ongoing:

> Homosexual identity formation is continuous, a process of "becoming" that spans a lifetime. . . . For this reason, commitment to the homosexual identity and role is a matter of degree. Homosexuals span a continuum from low to high levels of commitment on both internal and external dimensions, which may vary across time and place. Thus commitment is always somewhat inconsistent, strengthened, or weakened at various points and contexts by personal, social, or professional factors. (Troiden, 1989, p. 68)

Identity involves more than sexual expression. It is evident that a gay, lesbian, or bisexual orientation is not dependent, in either the adolescent or the adult, on one or multiple homosexual experiences. Many lesbian, gay, and bisexual youth may be sexually abstinent. Remafedi (1990, p. 1171) notes:

> It is a common misconception that adolescents cannot know they are lesbian or gay without first having pleasurable homosexual experiences and unsatisfactory heterosexual encounters. The suggestion of a sexual litmus test is especially perilous in light of the problems of adolescent pregnancy, abuse, sexually transmitted diseases, and acquired immunodeficiency syndrome (AIDS). Unfortunately, many youth are prodded to risk their physical and emotional health in order to resolve confusion. Sexual orientation might be more accurately and safely

assessed by their fantasies, emotional or romantic attractions, and identification with other heterosexual or homosexual persons.

Coles and Stokes (1985) reported that only one of 1,067 young people in a representative sample identified as homosexual by checking the appropriate box on their survey. They noted, however, that about five percent admitted in engaging in homosexual activity during adolescence. Remafedi, Resnick, Blum and Harris (1992), in a representative study of 34,706 Minnesota students in grades 7-12, found that 10.7 percent of students were unsure of their sexual orientation, 88.2 percent identified as primarily heterosexual, and 1.1 percent self-described as either bisexual or predominantly homosexual. Of note was that "the reported prevalence of homosexual attractions (4.5%) exceeded homosexual fantasies (2.6%), sexual behavior (1%), or affiliation (0.4%)" (p. 714).

These statistics may underestimate the populations of bisexual, lesbian, and gay young persons in the United States, but they certainly do not overestimate it. First, the stigma associated with identification as a member of any one of these populations is strong. Second, as has been demonstrated, full self-identification is often a lengthy process, which may not be completed until late adolescence or beyond. These, and other, factors mitigate against self-identification, even in anonymous surveys. The number or percentage of lesbian, gay male, and bisexual youth and young adults there are in the United States is likely to remain indeterminable for some time. Recent estimates of the percentage of homosexuals in the population as a whole range from as low as 2 percent to as high as 10 percent. Census data from the 1990 census reveal 5.4 percent of the total population to be in the 14-18 year-old age group, and 10.5 percent in the 18-24 year old age group. This 15.9 percent represents nearly 40,000,000 youth and young adults, more than 13,000,000 of whom were between 14 and 17 years old in 1990. Even if the number who are arguably lesbian or gay is assumed to be only two percent of all in their middle teens, there were approximately 267,000 lesbian or gay youth in this age group. That number grows to 1,333,500 at the least, if the truer proportion is ten percent.

Whatever the exact numbers, it is certain that lesbian, gay, and bisexual youth comprise a significant number of youth overall.

They face not only those developmental challenges faced by other young persons, but also a set of very special ones, as we have seen. Attention will now turn to some of those specific areas of need and concern which are particular to lesbian, gay, and bisexual youth.

EDUCATION

School and school-related activities comprise a major portion of adolescent life. Gay and lesbian students cope with stresses in addition to those encountered by their non-gay counterparts in school activities. These stresses, some of which are related to self-discovery in the process of identification, may interfere with school socialization, school success, and with the learning process itself. Sexual minority students are often subjected to varying degrees of harassment and overt abuse by other students, and the "keep quiet about this" handling of such incidents by school personnel may lead to an increased frequency of their occurrence.

Cook and Pawlowski (1991) suggest at least six important areas to address when considering the school environment for lesbians, gays, and bisexual adolescents:

1. Break the silence around homosexuality and bisexuality, and affirm diversity. This includes the visible placement of educational materials about gay and lesbian sexuality, including pamphlets, posters, and books.
2. Make the environment a safe one for sexual minority youth. Lesbian, gay, and bisexual youth may frequently be called names themselves, or may experience name-calling second hand. Schools need to foster an environment wherein sexually-harassing and discriminatory behavior is unacceptable, thus modeling for students an appreciation for diversity and the dignity and respect of all people. Abuse and harassment, whether physical or emotional, must simply neither be tolerated nor ignored. Additionally, schools must establish environments where it is safe for lesbian, gay, and bisexual adults to be as open about their orientation as it is for non-gay persons. Modeling by responsible adults will both lessen the negative impacts of self-discovery and aid in the creation of an

atmosphere free from discrimination and abuse. When such abuse does occur, in whatever form, school officials should act swiftly to protect the victimized adolescent, rather than ignore such behavior or, as has happened, punish the gay student with tacit approval of the aggression.

3. Teach adults working in schools and related institutions about human sexuality, and about homosexuality and bisexuality specifically. Included in such training should be topics geared toward reducing stigma and threats to the safety of youth. Cook and Pawlowski also suggest that the differences among the concepts of sexual orientation, sexual behavior, and sexual identity be clarified for personnel working with adolescents. Stigma-free language must be made familiar. Any such education must occur on an ongoing basis.

4. Include in curricula truthful information about known historic figures who were gay or lesbian or bisexual, who have contributed to the scientific, social, economic, political, and cultural richness that comes to us from the current and prior generations.

5. Include opportunities for parents of all youth in schools to learn more about the development of sexualities in their myriad forms. While clearly not all parents are the parents of gay youth, their children may nonetheless count lesbians, gay males, or bisexuals among their friends. Accepting, knowledgeable attitudes from parents, whether one's own or the parents of one's friends, make a positive difference to sexual minority young people. Parental educational opportunities should include training about general sexual development, stigma associated with homosexuality, psychosocial development in gay and non-gay youth, violence against gay youth, stereotyping, and cultural values impacting such youth.

6. Schools need to provide environmental and specific psychosocial support for bisexual, gay, and lesbian adolescents. In Los Angeles and San Francisco, specific programs exist for sexual minority youth. In San Francisco, schools have designated staff who are available to share students' concerns around their sexual orientation. In Los Angeles, at Fairfax High School, a special program (Project Ten) offers counsel-

ing and peer support groups for sexual minority youth. During its formation, sexual minority youth played an important role in the needs assessment process.

Teachers, coaches, and administrators play an important role in both mitigating or enhancing the negative effects of stressors associated with participation in school life. School boards may need to set standards addressing these issues. The school experience is germinal in the lives of sexual minority adolescents, and as such it must be made a highly positive one.

HEALTH ISSUES

Physical health and safety are important for all adolescents, and particularly for sexual minority youth. Substance use and abuse, as well as sexual activity, put youth today at particular risk for the transmission of a host of diseases, many life-threatening or potentially debilitating. These include chlamydia, gonorrhea, syphilis, yeast infections, hepatitis-B, HIV infection and AIDS, and others. Not all gay and lesbian youth are at higher risk for any of these than are other adolescents. For runaway and homeless sexual minority youth, however, some pose major threats to physical well-being. These youth may engage in survival sex, as well as alcohol and drug use, which puts them at high risk for contracting serious diseases. Some studies in metropolitan areas, such as Los Angeles, suggest that the percentage of runaway/homeless youth who are gay is between 25 and 40 percent of all such youth (Los Angeles County Task Force on Runaway and Homeless Youth, 1988; Seattle Commission on Children and Youth, 1988). It has also been well documented that there are large "clusters" of homeless runaway, throwaway and pushout gay and lesbian teens found in metropolitan areas of cities that have a sizable adult gay and lesbian population. Lesbian and gay youngsters appear to hold the mistaken belief that cities that are known to have a significant gay and lesbian population will provide an hospitable environment for them. In particular, these clusters are found in New York, San Francisco, Seattle, San Diego, and Los Angeles. The year round warm weather of the latter two cities seems to be an added draw. Moreover, survival sex puts such youth at higher risk of being raped, which anecdotal reports suggest happens often, both on the streets and in some shelters, particularly those which commingle younger adolescents with older, adult youth.

Access to preventive and restorative health care services may pose special difficulties for all sexual minority youth. There are significant social barriers to self-disclosure of sexual orientation and sexual behavior, and the reticence to disclose may impede the diagnosis and treatment of medical conditions. Youth may use denial and avoidance to escape detection by adults, which can result in their failure to seek necessary services. Other barriers to services include unavailability, cost, lack of transportation, risk of disclosure to significant others, and the inability of a given young person to follow through with appointments.

What are the medical problems that arise among gay male, lesbian, and bisexual youth? The limited literature suggests that the profiles differ significantly for males and females. Lesbians are seen as less at risk, their risk apparently being even less than that for heterosexual females (Robertson & Schachter, 1981). It is important to note that this study was conducted among adult women, whose risk factors are no doubt different from those of adolescent and young adult women. For example, many of the young lesbians found in group homes and at social service agencies specializing in serving this population may be users of street drugs (including injection use), and their risk factors are significantly higher than those factors might have been ten or fifteen years ago. This is an area in which considerable research is needed.

Sexual minority adolescents are not necessarily sexually active at all. However, as with young lesbians, those gay or bisexual males who have been pushed out of their homes, or who have run away or otherwise live "on the streets" tend to engage in sexual and drug use behaviors which place them at extremely high risk for contracting HIV and other diseases.

Remafedi (1985, p. 483-484) delineated four categories of sexually related illnesses found among gay males: "'classic' venereal diseases, viral illnesses, the 'gay bowel syndrome', and acquired immunodeficiency syndrome." Classic sexually transmitted diseases (STDs) include gonorrhea and pubic lice as the most common. Gonorrhea may be rectal, and go undetected for long periods of time, as can venereal throat infections. Scabies and syphilis are also found in this group. Associated viral disorders for which youth and young adults are at risk include herpes simplex virus (HSV), hepatitis A (HAV), hepatitis B (HBV), and hepatitis C (HCV), cytomegalovirus (CMV), and hepatitides, of which CMV is most prevalent in gay males, generally. In gay bowel syndrome, a number of infectious agents come into play (Quinn, Stamm, & Goodell, 1983). Such infections include campylobacter, shigella, chlamydia, amoebic pathogens, and giardiasis. Remafedi (1985) and Rosenfeld (1991) both recommend that the finding of one STD in an individual should lead health professionals to look for others as well.

Not surprisingly, these infections are associated with both high risk sexual behaviors and with drug use. Silvestre, Kingsley, Wehman, Dappen, Ho, and Rinaldo (1993) report on their study of 1614 gay and bisexual men, which spanned the years 1984-1985 and 1988-1992 in Pittsburgh, Pennsylvania. Sixteen percent of the men entering the study in 1988 reported having unprotected anal receptive intercourse with multiple partners in the six month period preceding their study visit. Seven percent of the participants under the age of 22 were already infected with the human immunodeficiency virus. This rate of infection was found to be equivalent to that in their first (1984-1985) cohort study, and provides compelling evidence that high school youth have a need for risk reduction programs.

The fourth, and final, category identified by Remafedi (1985) was that of HIV and AIDS with its many complications. In the study by Silvestre et al. (1993), researchers found that 18 percent of the gay and bisexual men over 22 years of age had positive tests for antibodies to HIV. Infection rates are even higher among gay and bisexual men of color (Schwarcz, Bolan, Kellogg, Kohn, & Lemp, 1993).

AIDS education is present in many school settings. Much of the material employed in some communities is focused on reaching the heterosexual youth population. While this focus may be inadvertent, it is important to consider the ramifications of non-gay oriented prevention programs for lesbian, gay, and bisexual youth, some of whom may be at far higher risk than their heterosexual counterparts. It would be easy to attribute this reality to homophobia on the part of teachers and parents. However, one of the major reasons may be due to the relative invisibility of these youth. Where the environment is hostile, or at least not overtly welcoming, fear and the need to hide mitigate against visibility. AIDS education and prevention efforts must target all youth and young people, including ethnic and sexual minorities.

Another problem with respect to AIDS prevention education has to do with how vague and abstract most of the mainstream educational efforts have been. Kristine Gebbie, the White House AIDS Coordinator, commented that "there has been some trouble because saying the word 'condom' is very upsetting to some people. As if kids don't know those words! They know a lot and they will have a hard time thinking of the things they need to know to enter adult life if we can't talk about them openly." Gebbie added that " . . . we need to target ads. In some cases ads need to be more explicit, in some cases maybe they could be less explicit" (New York Times, June 27, 1993).

Underscoring Gebbie's concerns, Dr. Debra Haffner, Executive Director of the Sexual Information and Education Council of the United States (SIECUS), says that while officials have been willing to talk about the disease in schools in recent years, the material is too abstract and fails to provide practical information because of a reluctance to discuss sexual matters clearly. A survey by her council showed that "children have not been taught the skills they need to reduce their risk, such as where to find condoms and how to use them." Haffner expressed her puzzlement at seeing a television commercial sponsored by the Centers for Disease Control and Prevention that showed a man putting on a sock, and the narrator saying, "If you could save your life by something as easy as putting on a sock, wouldn't you do it?" Haffner, who does sex education for a living, said, " I turned to my husband and said, 'What was that about?' It is hard to get people to adopt safer sex practices if one can't talk about it in ways that seem appealing" (New York Times, June 27, 1993). Clearly, these concerns are most urgent for high risk gay and lesbian youth, particularly those who are living out of home, whether in foster or group home care, in a residential treatment center, as part of the juvenile justice system, in a youth shelter, or on the streets. The challenge to give them the tools they need to prevent STDs including HIV disease is a daunting one, but one which must be met.

HIV infected youth encounter a particular set of predicaments, especially if they are under the age of 18. If they have already come into contact with the social services or criminal justice systems, and/or if living on the street, few or no services for health care, shelter, and food may be readily available. Until they are in the final stages of AIDS, hospital care will not be provided. Group homes and similar programs that are sensitive to and comfortable with lesbian, gay, bisexual, and other sexual minority youth, may be able to provide services as long as the adolescent is relatively healthy. But should the physical condition of the teen deteriorate, these same homes may be prohibited from providing food, clothing, shelter, and supportive treatment due to restrictions in licensing laws, or due to the attitudes of government agencies. Hospices may or may not have provisions for caring for adolescents. Even if hospice care were available, many youth would prefer to remain in more familiar surroundings with other youth, rather than entering a hospice populated by unfamiliar adults.

HIV and AIDS prevention strategies targeting lesbian, gay, bisexual, and other sexual minority youth are numerous. A recent study by Rotheram-Borus and Koopman (1991) points to the need not only for education, but also for empowerment. In a study of sexual risk behaviors, AIDS knowledge, and beliefs about AIDS prevention among ethnic minority adolescent males, the researchers found a striking contrast between the youth's moderately high level of HIV/ AIDS knowledge and beliefs about the effectiveness of AIDS prevention and their actual behavior. The study team associated the perception of a youth's *being in control* with the ability to avoid high risk behaviors. This, and related studies, suggest that enhanced self-efficacy and empowerment of youth must go hand-in-hand with AIDS education and prevention efforts if they are to be effective.

Another study by Koopman, Rotheram-Borus, Dobbs, Gwadz, and Brown (1992) asked 70 male and 59 female runaway youth in the New York City area what their responses would be if they found that they had contracted HIV. Twenty-nine percent reported that they would be self-destructive or hurt others (attempt suicide or have unprotected sex with others), 80 percent expected to experience extreme distress, forty-seven percent anticipated problems in finding food and shelter, and sixty-one percent thought that their friends would avoid them. However, when presented with a specific set of alternatives for support, fewer anticipated suicide. The researchers also discovered that drug use would be more likely to lead these youth to seek HIV testing than would sexual activity. The authors recommend that service providers anticipate the potential for self-destructive behaviors and emotional turmoil in similar groups, and that they be prepared to provide genuine access to needed services, including medical care, counseling, food and shelter.

Substance use among the young, while apparently decreasing overall among student populations, is still a major problem for many young gays, lesbians, bisexuals, and other sexual minority youth. Incidence rates are not readily determined, but certainly among homeless sexual minority youth the problems are significant. Since drug use may be associated with sexual activity as well as with non-conforming youth cultures, it is evident that adequate and sensitive services need to be made available to this particularly vulnerable population. They are not at present, at least not to a sufficient extent.

HOMELESS AND STREET YOUTH

While homeless and street youth are visible in urban areas, those among their numbers who are lesbian, gay, bisexual, or of another sexual minority are not readily determinable. Yates, Mackenzie, Pennbridge, and Swofford (1991) studied 620 homeless youth who utilized the services of an adolescent outpatient medical clinic over a 12-month period from July, 1988 through June, 1989. Of these, approximately six percent self-identified as homosexual, five percent identified as bisexual, and nearly two percent were undecided about their sexual orientation. Thus, about 13 percent of those in the study were gay or lesbian, bisexual, or undecided. This figure may be lower than the actual number due to possible reticence to report a non-heterosexual orientation, or due to any given adolescent not yet identifying her or his non-heterosexual orientation. Yates et al. note:

Youth involved in prostitution were more than five times as likely to report homosexual or bisexual identities. The age of first sex of these two groups also deserves comment. In this sample, 76% of the involved youth had sexual intercourse before age 15 years, and 26% had sex before their 10th birthday. (p. 547)

Runaway and homeless youth comprise most of the adolescents engaging in prostitution or survival sex. These activities significantly increase the likelihood of exposure to myriad sexually transmitted diseases, and may have contributed to the recent increase in the incidence of tuberculosis.

Prostitution and survival sex occur among both female and male sexual minorities. Somewhat telling is that much of the research has been focused on male homosexuals. What is known is that both boys and girls who engage in prostitution are likely to have been victims of abuse or neglect as children. Males tend to engage in same-sex sexual activities, which does not appear to be predominant among females (Schaffer & DeBlassie, 1984). Allen (1980) found a relationship between the type of prostitution and sexual orientation identity. In this study, the author found that call or kept boys[3] were the most likely to identify as homosexual (on the Kinsey scale), and that delinquent males who hustled for survival in bars or on the streets were the least likely to so identify. Fully half of Allen's sample identified as predominately homosexual, 28 percent identified as bisexual, and 19 percent as heterosexual. However, as Coleman (1989) suggests, "These results indicate that at least an incidental homosexual arousal or a psychic response or both is present in male juvenile prostitution, and most have more than an incidental homosexual response" (Kinsey 2-6) (p. 137).

There are high rates of substance use and abuse among homeless youth in general, and among those involved in prostitution in particular. In the study by Yates et al. (1991), researchers found that 74.5 percent of homeless youth who were engaging in prostitution also had diagnosable drug abuse problems, as compared to 36 percent of homeless youth who did not acknowledge engaging in prostitution. Lest we take comfort in this for non-prostituting youth, consider that over one-third of all youth in this study have drug abuse problems that were diagnosable!

Drugs of abuse for sexual minority youth living on the streets run the spectrum. However, in terms of cost and availability, crack (smokable rock cocaine), crystal methamphetamine (glass), marijuana, alcohol, and heroin are probably the leading drugs of choice. While any adolescent, including sexual minority youth, may experiment with or become a regular user of these substances, their use is almost routine among homeless youth. Drugs lessen the subjective pain of being alone and rejected, they decrease the sense of worthlessness many youth report, and they reduce inhibitions and guilt, which then enables the youth to engage in sexual activity for money despite how s/he might otherwise feel about prostitution. Finally, many drugs, particularly crack, are inexpensive, easily obtained, and both highly and quickly addicting.

Unfortunately, there are few social or medical services available to intervene in drug use among homeless youth. Much of the intervention occurs only at the level of the juvenile justice system, which itself is underfunded in most jurisdictions. Youth seeking treatment and recovery services often find themselves on waiting lists, if indeed services are available to them at all in the community. Those few services that do exist are often not gay affirming, primarily because gay and lesbian teens have learned to hide who they are. Thus, service providers do not always take the special needs of gay and lesbian adolescents into account when they plan and design programs. Among probation, children's services, and child protective services agencies in the public sector throughout the country, the gay and lesbian adolescent population has typically been underdefined, underestimated, underserved, and generally ignored.

Some larger cities, such as Los Angeles, Chicago, Washington, D.C., Boston, and New York do have social service agencies specifically designed to address some of these needs. Gay and Lesbian Adolescent Social Services (GLASS), which provides group and foster homes for sexual minority youth, is one such agency working with youth up to the age of 18. The Gay and Lesbian Community Services Center of Los Angeles (GLCSC) is another. The Center operates a transitional living program for homeless gay and lesbian youth, usually between the ages of 18 and 25. Horizons in Chicago, the Sexual Minority Assistance League (SMYAL) in Washington, D.C., the Boston Alliance of Gay and Lesbian Youth in Boston, and

Hettrick-Martin Institute in New York were all designed from the outset to meet the needs of sexual minority youth. All such programs, however, are overburdened and cannot address the needs of many street youth due to an insufficiency of resources. Foundation and government funding are difficult to obtain, and thus the needs of thousands of homeless lesbian, bisexual, gay and other sexual minority youth remain unmet.

SOCIAL ISSUES

Among the needs of all developing adolescents are opportunities for socialization with peers. This need is perhaps greater among gay, lesbian and bisexual youth, since school and church functions typically are not oriented towards any other than heterosexual youth. Thus, sexual minority youth do not have regular opportunities to socialize in an affirming, safe atmosphere. School activities, school dances, and even clubs, tend to be structured towards providing for the needs of heterosexual young people. As a result, lesbian and gay male adolescents are deprived of non-erotic socialization opportunities, where they can simply "be themselves."

Instead, out of a need to explore their orientation and identity, they are thrust into situations where the focus may be on sexual exploration and activity. While such exploration may be a part of maturation for all youth, it tends to be particularly secretive and even demeaning for young gays and lesbians. Lesbian and gay male adolescents can go out with same-identified friends, but at some risk of exposure and of taunting by non-gays. The opportunity to develop age-appropriate intimate friendships and dating relationships is not only difficult for these youth to find, but overtly denied to them by the institutions they must participate in. The peculiar phenomenon that occurs as a result of the absence of socializing opportunities is that gay and lesbian adolescents find themselves having to reach out to adults in order to find social gratification. This usually leads to premature sexual experiences, and sexual encounters that are not peer-experimentation and exploration. Rather, there is the power imbalance inherent in adult-adolescent sexual relationships. Worse, children find themselves having sexual intercourse before they have learned how to have social intercourse.

Thus, they are denied the opportunity to successfully complete the developmental tasks in what Erikson calls the "Identity vs. Confusion" stage of life. In his developmental model, Erikson notes that "so much of young love is conversation" (Erikson, 1968). The development of more opportunities for gay and lesbian adolescents to meet one another in appropriate social settings will remove much of the sexual pressure currently experienced by gay and lesbian teens.

Where they exist, gay and lesbian community centers and programs routinely offer youth programs with age-appropriate socialization activities. However, in many instances these programs are structured to serve older youth (18-23 years of age) only. Age limits exist at the upper end to protect older youth and young adults from the interference of those 24 years of age and older. But the services are unavailable in some areas for those under 18 because agencies don't want to face the harassment which might prevail should they be accused of "recruiting" youth to a "homosexual lifestyle." The myth of recruitment still abounds in many, particularly politically conservative and fundamentalist religious, circles.

VIOLENCE TOWARDS SEXUAL MINORITY YOUTH

Sexual minority adolescents and young adults, like their older counterparts, may be victims of familial and cultural violence. Familial violence is of at least two forms: physical or sexual abuse generally in the family system, and physical abuse as a result of disclosure of the adolescent's sexual orientation or identity conflicts.

Moreover, sexual minority youth, or youth thought by some others to be gay or lesbian, may be prime targets for anti-gay violence. Berrill (1990), Hunter (1990), and others have noted that this violence may be the result of increasing homophobia secondary to the HIV crisis. Berrill (1990) suggests that anti-gay violence (AGV) may also arise from organized hate groups and hate organizations. Berrill and Herek (1990) discuss some further implications for victims of this violence beyond physical injury. Sexual minorities often encounter lack of support or assistance from police officials. They may also lose jobs or housing as a secondary result of the violence. This is no less true for sexual minority youth. Such incidents may result in premature exposure to negative parental and peer response, before the youth is in a position to identify herself or himself in any particular way. This is a potential source of secondary violence to the young person.

In a retrospective study of clinical charts for the first 500 youth seeking services in 1988 at a New York City agency serving primarily lesbian and gay youth, Hunter reports that 40 percent had been physically attacked. She describes:

> The youths reporting violence did not differ significantly from the general sample of youths seeking services at the Hettrick-Martin Institute. Their mean age was 17.1; 21% of them were female; 42% were Black, 40% Latino, 16% White, and 2% other. Of those reporting violent physical assaults, 46% reported that the assault was gay-related; 61% of the gay-related violence occurred in the family. Suicidal ideation was found among 44% of those experiencing violent assaults: 41% of the girls and 34% of the boys reporting violent assaults had tried to kill themselves. (Hunter, 1990, p. 297)

Hunter points out that the majority of the youth in this study were ethnic minority, from working class backgrounds, and lesbian or gay–making them members of no fewer than three risk groups. The study is based on an existing convenience sample, so the results are not easily generalizable to a majority of gay youth. Nevertheless, the study of this clinical population may provide clues to the impact of AGV on non-clinically-involved gay and lesbian youth.

SUICIDALITY AND SUICIDE

Hunter (1990) suggests in her discussion that further research ought to look at connections between AGV and suicide among sexual minority adolescents. Other writers and researchers (Bell & Weinberg, 1978; Jay & Young, 1979; Kourany, 1987; Remafedi, 1987, 1991; Roesler & Deisher, 1972; U. S. Department of Health and Human Services [USDHHS], 1989) suggest that the suicidality of gay and lesbian youth is a major public health problem. Some suggest that being a lesbian or gay youth puts one at increased risk for suicidal behavior. These studies were conducted largely with gay and/or lesbian respondents, a number of whom were adults when the retrospective studies were conducted.

These studies, and many others, were examined and evaluated for inclusion in the 1989 USDHHS Report of the Secretary's Task Force on Youth Suicide. In one section of this report, Gibson (1989) reasonably argues that suicide is an issue impacting the well being of gay and lesbian youth. Writing several years later, David Shaffer, a psychiatrist and adolescent suicidologist (1993b), notes in an article in the *New Yorker* that most if not all of the studies cited by Gibson and others use convenience samples, which are known to be unrepresentative by their very nature. Shaffer argues that what is empirically known about youth suicide is that it tends to occur among several small groups of teens with particular attributes:

> The largest is a group of unpredictably aggressive, hotheaded males, who lose control with very little provocation. A second group is quite different: teen-agers who are chronically and irrationally anxious, and who may commit suicide just before some feared event. A third group consists of teen-agers who are simply clinically depressed; they see no good in themselves, and feel hopeless about the future. (p. 116)

While it is true that lesbian and gay youth do attempt suicide, Shaffer and others argue that the 1989 Task Force Report significantly overestimates the number of such attempts and completions. Careful examination of the data summarized in the report reveals that, indeed, most of the studies employed convenience samples of lesbians and gay men. As a result, projections predicated upon these studies may be misleading, since the samples are not representative of either gays, lesbians, bisexuals, nor of the general population of persons who have experienced suicidal ideation or engaged in suicidal behavior. Studies of adolescent suicide in general do not seem to support the notion that a high percentage of the victims are gay or lesbian.

Garrison, McKeown, Valois and Vincent (1993) surveyed 3,764 South Carolina public high school students for correlates of suicidal behavior. Using the 70-item Youth Risk Behavior Survey (a self-report measure), the researchers found that 25 percent of the students reported some sort of suicidal ideation or behavior, with females outnumbering males by about 1.5-2.0 to 1, somewhat lower than indicated in previous studies. Shaffer (1993a) notes that with regard to completed suicides (as distinguished from suicide attempts) among adolescents, males outnumber females by about 5 to 1. The study by Garrison et al. (1993) is a research milestone in adolescent suicidology, both with regard to the size of the sample and the researchers' methodology. It is the first large, in-depth study of a "general" adolescent population. Sexual orientation of surveyed youth was not addressed as a possible risk factor in this report, unfortunately. Additionally, the authors note:

> South Carolina is a predominantly rural state with a large minority population, mostly black. The population demographics are reflected in this study sample, especially given the nonparticipation of some school districts with lower non-white student enrollments. Although the number of white student participants was more than adequate for estimates by race and gender, the overall analysis may be limited in its applicability to populations who are more urban or more affluent or who have rather different ethnic constituencies. Furthermore, although the overall participation in the study was adequate, differential response could lead to selection bias and distorted results. (p. 182)

Garrison et al. (1993) did find significant relationships between substance use and suicidal behavior, and between aggressive behavior and suicidal behavior. Aggression and substance use or abuse may be a more important co-factor than depression in suicidal behavior among youth, including sexual minority youth. If the rate of such co-factors is higher among sexual minority youth than among youth generally, then sexual orientation may be another co-factor. However, such a relationship has yet to be empirically demonstrated.

While it is important to be aware of the particular risk factors with all depressed youth, it is essential that research about suicidality among gay and lesbian adolescents be limited to those youth with clear risk factors indicative of suicide potential in *any* youth or young adult. If we study a population of gay and lesbian youth in a clinical setting, such as an outreach program or mental health or social services agency, then we can only generalize to members of those groups, and not to sexual minority youth as a whole. Research limited to clinical populations, or to gay-, lesbian-, and bisexually-identified youth only, does not accurately reflect relative risks of suicide among those sexual minority youth.

Remafedi, Farrow, and Deisher (1991) conducted a systematic examination of suicide attempts among 137 gay male and bisexual male youth. The research participants were recruited over a one-year period in 1988 via advertising in gay periodicals, in bars, in social support groups for gay youth and university students, in a youth drop-in center, and by peer referral. None were referred from mental health treatment facilities. Participants were told that they were part of a study of gay and bisexual health issues for men age 21 and under. Factors predictive of such attempts in this study group were found to include gender nonconformity and precocious psychosexual development. Suicide attempters also, however, tended to resemble suicide victims generally. They tended to come from dysfunctional families, to be substance abusers, and to engage in other antisocial behaviors. The researchers also found that "for each year's delay in bisexual or homosexual self-labeling, the odds of a suicide attempt diminished by 80%."

It is premature to draw any firm conclusions from these diverse studies and attempt to apply them to all gay men, lesbians, bisexuals, or other sexual minorities. More research needs to be done in the area of gay and lesbian adolescents and suicidal behavior.

De Anda and Smith (1993) examined existing data on 165 adolescents from age 12 to 19, 65 young adults aged 20 to 26 years, and 175 adults aged 27 and older. These data were obtained on individuals who were callers to either a youth crisis line with adolescent peer counselors, or the crisis line run by a major metropolitan suicide prevention program. While not the focus of the research, the authors found that two (1.2 percent) of the 165 youth calling in gave homosexuality as the primary reason for the call. Of course, some youth may have been reluctant to state this as the reason for calling. Major reasons for suicidal ideation given by adolescent callers included marital/love problem, family conflict, and abortion/pregnancy. Of these, the first two might mask a concern or conflict over sexual orientation. However, the best information available from this study is that homosexuality is not a major presenting issue to youth calling crisis lines.

In a report summarizing national studies on youth hotlines and crisis lines, Howard (1993) interviewed hot line service providers and youth workers. Overall, it appears that such hotlines may do little to curb suicide. People intent on suiciding, including youth, may not call the hotlines. However, some preventative effects may nonetheless be provided by the lines, in offering referrals for counseling and other services to troubled youth before their lives become unmanageable to the point that suicide is an actively considered alternative. This report also suggests that local and state programs organized to prevent suicide by offering information broadly to students in classrooms may be counterproductive. In such programs, students are often given detailed information about other adolescents' suicides. Many professionals fear that such an approach may tend to "normalize" suicide as an alternative among youth, thus inadvertently perpetuating or encouraging it as somehow a useful, if desperate, choice.

Groze and Proctor (1993) reported on an international survey conducted the previous year regarding suicidality among gay, lesbian, and bisexual youth. They gathered data from 221 sexual minority youth. Nearly two-thirds of the adolescents participating in their study reported that they had either attempted or considered suicide (66.1%). In detail, 40.3 % had attempted suicide, 25.8% had seriously thought about it at least once, and 33.9% had neither made an attempt nor thought about it.

The implications of this research are limited by the skewness of the sample, since all of the subjects had received at least one contact with a gay, lesbian, and bisexual youth group, which, according to the authors' executive summary of the results, may have affected the isolation that the youth frequently feel. Further, only youth who are familiar with these urban groups as a resource were included in the study. Obviously, the sample is not entirely representative of the population who were the target of the study. Nonetheless, the authors offer insight into the high suicide risk to those sexual minority youth who seek help from social service agencies.

Herdt and Boxer, in 1993, reported on a study conducted among youth who were part of Horizons (a lesbian and gay social service agency in Chicago). Twenty-nine percent of their total sample reported at least one suicide attempt prior to entering the Horizons' youth group. More than half of the sample of lesbian teenagers, as compared to 20 percent of the gay males, reported at least one attempt. Despite the study findings of alarmingly high rates of suicidality among these youth, the study participants compared favorably overall with adolescents at large in their psychological resilience and distress. They also did not reveal major differences in anxiety, confusion, and insecurity when compared to adolescents in general, though some did tend to be more depressed, vigilant and vulnerable when compared to heterosexual peers.

Hammelman (1993) reported on a survey of forty-eight gay, lesbian, or bisexual youth in Iowa. Participants in the study either attended a support group in Des Moines, or participated in campus activities planned for this population at Iowa State University in Ames, Iowa. Non-probability, purposive sampling served as the method to obtain respondents for this study, who were selected in part because of the ease of access to them. The youth were administered a questionnaire, which consisted of eighteen close-ended questions. Of those completing questionnaires, 29% had attempted suicide, evenly divided between males and females. Seventy-one percent of those who had attempted suicide did so prior to age 17.

Nearly half of the respondents (44%) stated that they had been verbally, physically, or sexually abused, while more than half (53%) cited sexual orientation as part or the main reason for the abuse they suffered. Thirty-five percent of the respondents admitted to a drug or alcohol problem, and more than half of them (59%) viewed sexual orientation as part or the main reason for their substance abuse problem. Rejection by family members was reported by twenty-three percent of the participants, seventy percent of whom indicated that sexual orientation was part or the main reason for the rejection.

Hammelman concluded that "gay and lesbian youth are at risk for suicide if they (1) discover their same sex preference early in adolescence, (2) experience violence due to their gay or lesbian identity, (3) use drugs or alcohol to cope with problems regarding their sexual orientation and (4) are rejected by family members as a result of being lesbian or gay" (p. 84-85).

Generally, studies of sexual minority youth and suicide fail to definitively support either the thesis that such youth are inherently at higher risk for suicide, or the thesis that they are more likely to complete a suicide attempt. Shaffer (1993b) argues that data from many convenience samples have been used by both pro- and anti-gay forces to argue for specific political goals. He argues that such use is inappropriate because of the nature of the convenience samples.

Such studies cannot be proffered as proof that sexual minority adolescents, as a group, are at greater suicide risk. They do illustrate the need for the inclusion of items pertaining to sexual orientation in any survey of adolescents generally. Even so, the fluidity of sexual identity, sexual orientation, and sexual behavior during adolescence gives rise to problems in ascertaining accurately which respondents are lesbian, gay, or bisexual. Moreover, studies involving psychological autopsies of completed adolescent suicides must include such questions.

Further research into the relationship between adolescents' sexual orientation and suicide, while posing methodological difficulties, is an essential undertaking before accurate generalizations can be established. It is unfortunate that the study by Garrison et al. (apparently) did not consider sexual orientation as a possible co-factor relating to adolescent suicidal ideation and behavior. Future researchers would do well to consider this additional variable, and research which includes more urban adolescent populations would be valuable.

CONCLUSION

This paper has been an effort to review generally what is known about a number of issues involving gay, lesbian, bisexual and other sexual minority youth, including their developmental issues. From the outset, the relative paucity of empirical or qualitative information available about this population was discouraging.

There are at least several predominant concerns affecting lesbian, gay, and bisexual youth. First, teachers, recreation workers, clergy, and social/medical/mental health service providers need to be aware of the issues impacting these youth. Second, professionals must sensitize themselves to the risk issues these youth face. Third, further research is essential to explore the factors associated with gay and lesbian adolescents who master developmental challenges and stages with relative comfort, and we must study the factors impacting those who respond to such challenges with antisocial and self-destructive behavior. Until such research is funded, professionals and laypersons are at risk of maintaining a focus on problems rather than solutions, and those solutions that are focused on will not necessarily be well-informed, as the discussion of suicide "hotlines" revealed. All lesbian, gay and bisexual youth deserve dignity, respect, nurture, and the freedom to be fully the persons whom they are, and they are entitled to sufficient support from societal systems to enable them to achieve their fullest potential as adults. As service providers, parents, teachers, researchers, and clergy, whether we are lesbian, gay, bisexual or heterosexual, we have a responsibility to make their world as accepting of them as possible, and to model responsible caring behavior.

NOTES

1. "Other sexual minority" includes transvestites and transsexual youth. While there is little research extant on these phenomena in teens and young adults, programs working with sexual minority youth have identified them and include consideration of their needs when developing services.

2. Homophobia has taken on a number of meanings. Smith (1971) described it as an irrational fear of homosexuality that is all-pervasive in society. Remafedi (1990, p. 1172) suggests that it is of at least two forms: "Externalized," as a form of "prejudice or overt hostility towards homosexual persons; it may be embodied in self-defeating and self-compromising behaviors of homosexual persons themselves" (or *internalized*). He further notes: "Expressions of externalized and internalized homophobia are more pronounced during adolescence than at other times in the life cycle."

3. Call boys are those who are typically contacted by telephone, do not "work" the streets or hustler bars. Kept boys are those who typically live with an adult male who provides for their basic needs, recreation, spending money, transportation, etc., in exchange for companionship and/or sexual contact.

REFERENCES

Allen, D. M. (1980). Young male prostitutes: A psychosocial study. *Archives of Sexual Behavior, 9,* 399-426.

Bell, A. P., & Weinberg, M. S. (1978). *Homosexualities: A study of diversity among men and women.* New York: Simon and Schuster.

Bell, A. P., Weinberg, M. S., & Hammersmith, S. K. (1981a). *Sexual preference: Its development in men and women.* Bloomington, IN: Indiana University Press.

Bell, A. P., Weinberg, M. S., & Hammersmith, S. K. (1981b). *Sexual preference: Its development in men and women: Statistical appendix.* Bloomington, IN: Indiana University Press.

Berrill, K. T. (1990). Anti-gay violence and victimization in the United States: An overview. Special Issue: Violence against lesbians and gay men: Issues for research, practice, and policy. *Journal of Interpersonal Violence, 5*(3), 274-294.

Berrill, K. T., & Herek, G. M. (1990). Primary and secondary victimization in anti-gay hate crimes: Official response and public policy. Special Issue: Violence against lesbians and gay men: Issues for research, practice, and policy. *Journal of Interpersonal Violence, 5*(3), 401-413.

Cass, V. C. (1979). Homosexual identity formation: A theoretical model. *Journal of Homosexuality, 4,* 219-235.

Coleman, E. (1982). Developmental stages of the coming-out process. In W. Paul, J. D. Weinrich, J. C. Gonsiorek, & M. E. Hotvedt (Eds.), *Homosexuality: Social, psychological, and biological issues* (pp. 149-158). Beverly Hills, CA: Sage Publications.

Coles, R., & Stokes, G. (1985). *Sex and the American teenager.* New York: Harper & Row.

Cook, A. T., & Pawlowski, W. (1991). Youth and homosexuality. *Issue Paper 3.* Washington, DC: Parents and Friends of Lesbians and Gays.

Cronin, D. M. (1974). Coming out among lesbians. In E. Goode, & R. R. Troiden (Eds.), *Sexual deviance and sexual deviants* (pp. 268-277). New York: William Morrow & Sons.

Dank, B. M. (1971). Coming out in the gay world. *Psychiatry, 34,* 180-197.

de Anda, D., & Smith, M. A. (1993). Differences among adolescent, young adult, and adult callers of suicide help lines. *Social Work, 38*(4), 421-428.

Garrison, C. Z., McKeown, R. E., Valois, R. S., & Vincent, M. L. (1993). Aggression, substance use, and suicidal behaviors in high school students. *American Journal of Public Health, 83*(2), 179-184.

Gibson, P. (1989). Gay male and lesbian youth suicide. In *Report of the Secretary's task force on youth suicide, Volume 3: Prevention and interventions in youth suicide.* Rockville, MD: U. S. Department of Health and Human Services, pp. 3-110–3-142.

Groze, V., & Proctor, C. D. Unpublished "executive summary" of findings, 1993. Contact Curtis D. Proctor, 501 5th Street, Coralville, LA 52241.

Hammelman, T. L. (1993). Gay and lesbian youth: Contributing factors to serious attempts or considerations of suicide. *Journal of Gay & Lesbian Psychotherapy*, Vol. 2(1). New York: The Haworth Press, Inc.

Hammersmith, S. K. (1987). A sociological approach to counseling homosexual clients and their families. *Journal of Homosexuality, 14*, 173-190.

Harry, J., & DeVall, W. (1978). *The social organization of gay males*. New York: Praeger.

Herdt, G., & Boxer, A. (1993). *Children of Horizons*. Boston, MA: Beacon Press.

Howard, B. (1993). Suicidal youth: Hotlines don't work. *Youth Today: The Newspaper on Youth Work, 2*(3), 1, 26-27.

Humphreys, L. (1972). *Out of the closets: The sociology of homosexual liberation*. Englewood Cliffs, NJ: Prentice-Hall.

Hunter, J. (1990). Violence against lesbian and gay male youths. Special Issue: Violence against lesbians and gay men: Issues for research, practice, and policy. *Journal of Interpersonal Violence, 5*(3), 295-300.

Kooden, H. D., Morin, S. F., Riddle, D. L., Rogers, M., Strang, B. E., & Strassburger, F. (1979). *Removing the stigma: Final report of the board of social and ethical responsibility for psychology's task force on the status of lesbian and gay male psychologists*. Washington, DC: American Psychological Association.

Koopman, C., Rotheram-Borus, M. J., Dobbs, L., Gwadz, M., & Brown, J. (1992). Beliefs and behavioral intentions regarding human immunodeficiency virus testing among New York City runaways. *Journal of Adolescent Health, 13*(7), 576-581.

Kourany, R. F. Suicide among homosexual adolescents. *Journal of Homosexuality, 13*, 331-337.

Kruks, G. (1991). Gay and lesbian homeless/street youth: Special issues and concerns. *Journal of Adolescent Health, 12*(7), 515-518.

Los Angeles Task Force on Runaway and Homeless Youth. (1988). *Report and recommendations of the task force*. Los Angeles, CA: Author.

Malyon, A. K. (1982). Biphasic aspects of homosexual identity formation. *Psychotherapy: Theory, Research and Practice, 19*(3), 335-340.

McDonald, G. J. (1982). Individual differences in the coming out process for gay men: Implications for theoretical models. *Journal of Homosexuality, 8*, 47-60.

Quinn, T. C., Stamm, W. E., & Goodell, S. E. (1983). The polymicrobial origin of intestinal infections in homosexual men. *New England Journal of Medicine, 309*, 576-582.

Remafedi, G. (1985). Adolescent homosexuality. *Clinical Pediatrics, 24*(9), 481-485.

Remafedi, G. (1987). Male homosexuality: The adolescent's perspective. *Pediatrics, 79*(3), 326-330.

Remafedi, G. (1990). Fundamental issues in the care of homosexual youth. *Adolescent Medicine, 74*(5), 1169-1179.

Remafedi, G., Farrow, J. A., & Deisher, R. W. (1991). Risk factors for attempted suicide in gay and bisexual youth. *Pediatrics, 87*(6), 869-875.

Remafedi, G., Resnick, M., Blum, R., & Harris, L. (1992). Demography of sexual orientation in adolescents. *Pediatrics, 89*(4), 714-721.

Riddle, D. I., & Morin, S. F. (1977, November). Removing the stigma: Data from individuals. *APA Monitor, 16*, 28.

Robertson, P., & Schachter, J. (1981). Failure to identify venereal disease in a lesbian population. *Sexually Transmitted Diseases, 8*, 75-76.

Roesler, T., & Deisher, R. W. (1972). Youthful male homosexuality. *JAMA, 219*, 1018-1023.

Rosenfeld, W. D. (1991). Sexually transmitted diseases in adolescents: Update 1991. *Pediatric Annals, 20*(6), 303-312.

Rotheram-Borus, M. J., & Koopman, C. (1991). Sexual risk behavior, AIDS knowledge, and beliefs about AIDS among predominantly minority gay and bisexual male adolescents. *AIDS Education and Prevention, 3*(4), 305-312.

Rotheram-Borus, M. J., Koopman, C., & Ehrhardt, A. A. (1991). Homeless youths and HIV infection. Special Issue: Homelessness. *American Psychologist, 46*(11), 1188-1197.

Savin-Williams, R. C. (1990). *Gay and lesbian youth: Expressions of identity.* NY: Hemisphere Publishing Corporation.

Schäfer, S. (1976). Sexual and social problems among lesbians. *The Journal of Sex Research, 12*, 50-69.

Schaffer, B., & DeBlassie, R. R. (1984). Adolescent prostitution. *Adolescence, 19*(75), 689-696.

Schwarcz, S. K., Bolan, G. A., Kellogg, T. A., Kohn, R., & Lemp, G. F. (1993). Comparison of voluntary and blinded human immunodeficiency virus type 1 (HIV-1) seroprevalence surveys in a high prevalence sexually transmitted disease clinic population. *American Journal of Epidemiology, 137*(6), 600-608.

Seattle Commission on Children and Youth. (1988). *Report on gay and lesbian youth in Seattle.* Seattle, WA: City of Seattle, Department of Human Resources.

Shaffer, D. (1993). Suicide risk factors and the public health (Editorial). *American Journal of Public Health, 83*(2), 171-172.

Shaffer, D. (1993, May 3). Political science (quasi-scientific reports on suicidal behavior of gays cited to support ban on gays in military). *The New Yorker*, p. 116.

Silvestre, A. J., Kingsley, L. A., Wehman, P., Dappen, R., Ho, M., & Rinaldo, C. R. (1993). Changes in HIV rates and sexual behavior among homosexual men, 1984 to 1988/92. *American Journal of Public Health, 83*(4), 578-580.

Troiden, R. R. (1979). Becoming homosexual: A model of gay identity acquisition. *Psychiatry, 42*, 362-373.

Troiden, R. R. (1984/1985). Self, self-concept, identity, and homosexual identity: Constructs in need of definition and differentiation. *Journal of Homosexuality, 10*, 97-109.

Troiden, R. R. (1988). Homosexuality identity development. *Journal of Adolescent Health Care, 9*(2), 105-113.

Troiden, R. R. (1989). The formation of homosexual identities. *Journal of Homosexuality, 17*(1-2), 43-73.

Troiden, R. R., & Goode, E. (1980). Variables related to the acquisition of a gay identity. *Journal of Homosexuality, 5,* 383-392.

U. S. Department of Health and Human Services. (1989). *Report of the Secretary's task force on youth suicide, Volume 3: Prevention and interventions in youth suicide.* Rockville, MD: Author.

Warren, C. A. B. (1974). *Identity and community in the gay world.* New York: John Wiley & Sons.

Yates, G. L., Mackenzie, M. D., Pennbridge, J., & Swofford, A. (1991). A risk profile comparison of homeless youth involved in prostitution and homeless youth not involved. *Journal of Adolescent Health, 12*(7), 545-548.

Gay and Lesbian Youth:
Challenging the Policy of Denial

Nancy Taylor

SUMMARY. Social policy tends to reflect community standards regarding a population's individual rights, expected conduct, and entitlement to public services. Populations, therefore, must be defined and acknowledged by their communities and by their policy makers if they are to be included in these codified standards. Lesbian and gay youth have yet to be clearly defined as a population. The origins and subsequent development of the current lesbian and gay movement offer a framework in which to consider future efforts to change social policy regarding lesbian and gay youth. The lesbian and gay community, despite the significant loss of leadership and experience as the result of AIDS, has continued its development as a force for social change. Organizations such as Parents and Friends of Lesbians and Gays, and other groups focused on combatting bigotry and expanding civil rights, are of crucial importance to the future of lesbian and gay youth and to the development of enlightened policy. The sooner enlightened policies are developed, the sooner these youngsters will be able to lead happier, healthier, and more productive lives.

Few of the policy debates prior to 1985 regarding either the status of children or of lesbians and gays directly addressed the

Nancy Taylor, LCSW, has worked in both the public and private sectors, providing services to children and families since 1979. She has an extensive background in policy and public health, and has taught social policy in Hawaii, where she has resided for the past fourteen years.

[Haworth co-indexing entry note]: "Gay and Lesbian Youth: Challenging the Policy of Denial." Taylor, Nancy. Co-published simultaneously in *Journal of Gay & Lesbian Social Services* (The Haworth Press, Inc.) Vol. 1, No. 3/4, 1994, pp. 39-73; and: *Helping Gay and Lesbian Youth: New Policies, New Programs, New Practice* (ed: Teresa DeCrescenzo) The Haworth Press, Inc., 1994, pp. 39-73. Multiple copies of this article/chapter may be purchased from The Haworth Document Delivery Center [1-800-3-HAWORTH; 9:00 a.m. - 5:00 p.m. (EST)].

status of gay and lesbian youth (Licata and Petersen, 1985). Even the concept of gay children continues to be foreign to many policy makers and community members. However, increasing visibility of lesbians and gays has expanded public debate regarding homosexual rights to include the concerns of lesbian and gay youth. In fact, increasingly serious policy consideration of these issues has occurred during the last five years (Berzon, 1992).

There have been two general trends in policy change efforts regarding lesbian and gay youth since the late 1970s (Herdt, 1989; Marcus, 1992). In one arena, lesbian/gay youth advocates have pressed for policy and program changes within youth-serving institutions that would reflect increasing tolerance of, and support for, lesbian and gay youth and families. In another arena, lesbian and gay youth advocates have pressed lesbian and gay community organizations to develop services for, and seek funding on behalf of, lesbian and gay youth.

Social policy tends to reflect "community standards" regarding a population's individual rights, expected conduct, and entitlement to public services (Levine, 1991). Populations, therefore, must be defined and acknowledged by their communities and by their policy makers if they are to be included in these codified standards. Lesbian and gay youth have yet to be clearly defined as a population. However, they have begun to be recognized within the lesbian and gay community, by their parents and friends, and by organizations such as Parents and Friends of Lesbians and Gays, as well as by youth-serving professionals and organizations (Reiss-Davis, 1993; Hiratsuka, 1993).

DEFINING HOMOSEXUALITY
AND HOMOSEXUAL YOUTH

Homosexuality is increasingly being viewed as a complex phenomenon extending beyond behavior alone (Hooker, 1963; Clark, 1987; Bell and Weinberg, 1978). No longer classified as pathology, homosexuality is generally seen as a state of being, or a characteristic of the "self." These new definitions helped to change social policy by redefining "community standards" to normalize homosexuals as an authentic, discrete, and definable minority group.

Thus, homosexual adults could begin to successfully challenge social policy that previously codified discrimination against lesbians and gays. Protection of lesbian and gay youth from discrimination has followed a similar course, but has progressed much more slowly.

In many areas, recognition of the existence of gays and lesbians between the ages of 13 and 18 is limited to specialized sectors such as child welfare and probation departments (Duffy, 1992). Some high schools and many youth groups, such as the Boy Scouts of America, are still the sites of official discrimination, frequent hazing and taunting directed at lesbian and gay youth (see report on "Boy Scout Bigotry," 1991; Harbeck, 1992). Children under 13 are usually assumed to be developing as heterosexuals. They are also generally expected to be protected, at a minimum, from information concerning homosexuality and, some would argue, from the presence of homosexuals (Lacayo, 1992; Krauthammer, 1993). Lesbian and gay youth over age 18 can be found in large numbers in institutions such as the military, and in colleges and universities. They are vulnerable to discrimination to varying degrees, depending on the policies embraced by these institutions.

Since youth who are confused about their sexual orientation, and those who are afraid to self-disclose are defined as heterosexual by default, the only recognized lesbian and gay youth are those who publicly self-identify. As a result, it is impossible to determine exactly how many gay and lesbian youngsters there are, and the only clearly defined lesbian/gay youngsters are older than 13. There is no concrete evidence that children below 13 could be defined as homosexual though there is evidence that sexual orientation probably forms sometime in early childhood, and tends toward immutability by the end of the latency period. Many parents and others fear that young children might be recruited or seduced into homosexuality if exposed to homosexuals, or even to "permissive" attitudes regarding homosexuality, though there is no evidence to support such concern (Burr, 1993). If there is a definable population of lesbian/gay children under the age of 13, these younger children face markedly more denial of their existence than do their elders. They also face potentially more abuse if parents or teachers try to enforce social conformity. Efforts to coerce gender role conformity in elementary and pre-school children, for instance, are often expressions of homophobia (Fricke, 1991). Parental fear may also prevent youngsters from having accurate information about homosexuality, and thus contribute to the development of low self-esteem should homosexual impulses surface in adolescence. There is variance in these attitudes across cultural lines, though parental homophobia is the general theme.

The future of gay and lesbian youth is closely tied to that of gay and lesbian adults. The lesbian and gay adult civil rights movement created a more accepting climate for homosexuals. That climate eventually allowed attention to focus on gay and lesbian youth. Once recognized, the needs and experiences of gay and lesbian youth can be clarified through further social research and through social policy debate. Much of the research has been directed at defining homosexuality and quantifying the homosexual minority. Various definitions now include a 'lifestyle', a 'behavior(s)', a 'proven proclivity', a 'process of self-identification', and some newer, more 'scientific' descriptions based on genetic, developmental, and hormonal studies. Establishing policy for a population that cannot be readily defined is daunting. Policy debate becomes even more complex if the size of the population cannot be readily measured. For instance, a study by the Alan Guttmacher Institute, released in April, 1993, challenged the 40-year-old estimate by Kinsey that approximately 10% of the population is homosexual (Kinsey, 1948). Later that same year, a University of Hawaii researcher, Milton Diamond, released details of a study he conducted, which estimates that five percent of the population is gay or lesbian (FRONTIERS, September 10, 1993). If policy makers don't know the size of the population or who are its members, policy debate can become highly speculative. For instance, it is very difficult to allocate resources and services to the population to determine what protections the population needs and to ascertain the size and influence of the constituency base for them. Of course, these "numbers games" can also be used to justify establishing social policies that limit services.

HISTORY

Absent this information, policy debate can become distorted by prejudice, bigotry, and demagoguery. Lesbian and gay youth may be among the most difficult populations to define and quantify, thus further impeding policy considerations of their issues. They inhabit a sociological "no man's land." They live in heterosexual families and school settings where they are either rejected or unrecognized. They have little access to the adult lesbian and gay community, and rarely do they know other lesbian and gay youth. In addition, since they are still developing, their adult identities (including sexual identities) have yet to fully form. They are difficult to assist, in part, because even they have difficulty articulating and defining their needs. Thus, the task of developing policies, and the services which flow from policy, for lesbian and gay youth is potentially more prone to distortion by polarized interest groups.

The history of the lesbian and gay rights movement has had significant impact on the development of the current generation of lesbian and gay youth. Though individually isolated, these young people have been surrounded by an adult milieu in which the social policy debate concerning their sexuality has been increasingly public and polarized since 1969. The gay rights movement, in a public sense, is generally thought to have begun in 1969, with the Stonewall rebellion in New York City. The movement grew steadily, but comparatively quietly, until the mid-1970s. The heavily publicized debate over gay rights that many now associate with the "Gay Rights Movement" began in response to Anita Bryant's crusade against homosexuals.

In 1977, when the media did not readily discuss homosexuality in public, Ms. Bryant brought the subject to the public forum in a way that the homosexual movement had been unable. Her efforts to create anti-gay policies in Florida, and later nationwide, literally frightened many homosexuals out of hiding. Many became political activists, joined or helped to establish groups to challenge the "scapegoat" status of gays and lesbians in America. The political efforts to stop Ms. Bryant's national campaign and the concurrent fight against the anti-gay "Briggs Initiative" in California, evolved into a sophisticated gay and lesbian civil rights movement, as well as an organized, visible community of lesbians and gay men.

Any child born after 1975 has grown up in an era of public debate about homosexuality in which an organized, politicized community of lesbians and gays actively and successfully participates. Though the reactive origins of this movement are not widely discussed, the movement continues partly in response to sophisticated successors of Bryant and Briggs. Now identified as the "religious right," the opposition is determined to codify discrimination against homosexuals. In this climate, policy debates become distorted by rhetoric, and research data are manipulated to support positions (Los Angeles Times, August 22, 1993).

This group of youngsters, now 18, is the first population of gay and lesbian youth to have had such an experience. Over the years these debates have involved misinterpreted research data, vigorously expressed bigotry, vacillating public opinion regarding the need for gay rights, and the impact of AIDS on the emerging lesbian and gay community. These youngsters can identify with successful adult lesbian and gay role models, where previous generations of gays and lesbians grew up in an atmosphere of secrecy and silence, where all social policy involving homosexuals was punitive.

THE CURRENT SOCIOPOLITICAL SCENE

The origins, and the subsequent development of the current lesbian and gay movement, offer a framework in which to consider future efforts to change social policy regarding lesbian and gay youth. Neither policy makers nor advocates today operate within the context of denial regarding homosexuality. However, virtually all adults today matured during the era of silence. Policy makers who grew up unable to discuss homosexual issues now find themselves immersed in debate that is often shrill and distorted. In this climate, concerns about gay and lesbian youth are often set aside, or are lost in a fog of rhetoric.

In fact, the issues for policy consideration concerning lesbian and gay youth today retain much of the shroud, naivete and denial that once plagued the larger issue of homosexuality. While social policy changes regarding homosexuality overall have had profound effects on, and implications for, gay and lesbian youth, the unique needs of these youth have yet to be addressed. It is likely that efforts to define and describe their special needs will be accompanied by increasingly intense public debate.

Those seeking changes in social policy will strategically apply pressure from high-level policy makers within the lesbian and gay movement, a tactic which has often proven effective in minority advocacy. Sometimes this approach can result in rapid change with minimal controversy. Since the organized lesbian and gay community of the nineties has more allies and experience than in the past, once mobilized on behalf of lesbian and gay youth, advocates can press for change more efficiently than in the past (Boxall and Gerstenzang, 1993; DeCrescenzo, 1993).

Lesbian and gay youth today belong to a larger community that did not exist for their predecessors, a community organized in a political context. Thus, one of the most difficult tasks required to successfully advocate for any issue has already been accomplished, that of coalescing a dispersed, invisible, stigmatized population into an organized, identifiable, politically astute community which has its own institutions and advocacy groups (Goffman, 1963). An organized, identifiable community can lobby, form coalitions, and advocate for policies. There is clearly a need for specific social policy regarding lesbian and gay youth.

Unlike youth of 20 years ago, lesbian and gay youth today have lesbian and gay adults to speak for their needs in addition to, or perhaps irrespective of, whatever position their parents may have regarding their homosexuality. While under the age of 18, children have virtually no rights independent of their parents or legal guardians (Kaus, 1993). Few adults advocate for their lesbian or gay child, or for lesbian and gay children in general. Efforts on behalf of these youth by the organized lesbian and gay community may help mobilize the children's parents and friends, as well, to insure that lesbian and gay youth are protected from "vigilante" or institutional abuse and discrimination (Norris, 1992; Muther, 1993). (See elsewhere in this volume for a complete discussion of legal challenges faced by minor gay and lesbian youth.)

Lesbian and gay adults have the task of educating parents and guardians on behalf of lesbian and gay youth, as well as the task of lobbying directly for policy changes for these youth. Despite years of public debate, stigma still exists for homosexuals. Many people dismiss the idea of identifying children, or even allowing children to self-identify as lesbian or gay. Thus, lesbian and gay children endure denial within their private milieu, despite the frequent public debate about homosexual issues. Though lesbian and gay children can be profoundly affected by the character of this debate, they are often personally isolated and unable to discuss their feelings openly. Some of the most mean spirited public discourse has focused on the status of children vis á vis homosexuality, thus bringing lesbian and gay youth into a debate in which they have no voice.

These debates often concern the effect of homosexual adults upon children. In this context, lesbians and gays have been accused of "recruiting" children to be gay, of being pedophiles, and of encouraging homosexuality by serving as role models for children. Such accusations tend to dissuade homosexual adults from attempting to address the needs of lesbian and gay youth. They also portend a future role in which lesbian and gay youth may see themselves as society's undesirables. Additionally, such ill-founded arguments impede rational policy development, at the precise time that rational policy is desperately needed.

Gay and lesbian organizations have historically tended to shun lesbian and gay youth during the early years of the gay rights movement, fearing the perception that homosexual adults are preoccupied with recruiting or enticing children into homosexual behavior. Thus, until recently, the lesbian and gay community was largely a community of adults which had limited focus on children's issues, though many lesbians and gays have been concerned about the needs of children. In addition to lesbian and gay professionals involved with children as teachers, pediatricians and social workers, gays and lesbians are also parents and guardians. Thus, they are naturally concerned with children's issues, including concern for the needs of lesbian and gay youngsters specifically.

The population of publicly recognized gay/lesbian parents increased dramatically when artificial insemination became widely available during the late 1980s and early 1990s (Hitchens, 1991). This increase tended to lessen fears of the "recruitment" accusations, as more evidence surfaced that lesbians and gays are able, responsible parents and child-centered professionals (Ricketts and Achtenberg, 1990). In addition, parallel movements concerned about child abuse revealed that pedophilia is much more common among heterosexual males than among any other group. Finally, increasing evidence that sexual orientation forms in early childhood has further undermined arguments that lesbian and gay role models encourage homosexuality in young children. As they have become less frightened of accusations of child molestation or recruitment, lesbian and gay child advocates and their non-gay supporters have lobbied for policy changes in schools, children's groups, and child welfare agencies, as well as for inclusion of lesbian and gay families in family policy considerations (Harbeck, 1992).

There continues to be significant opposition to policy revision, especially as regards school curricula and the definition of family. The opposition forces in these areas found a voice in Dan Quayle's "family values" campaign in 1992 (DaFoe-Whitehead, 1993). In 1993, formal opposition again surfaced in the form of Pat Robertson's support of a campaign to rescind curricula that is accepting of homosexuality in New York public schools.

Efforts resisting policies that support lesbian and gay youth and families do not go unopposed. Lesbian and gay youth have been particularly supported by the efforts of increasingly visible numbers of gay and lesbian teachers. These groups have courageously lobbied for curriculum changes, and have helped establish services for lesbian and gay youth within some schools. Project 10 in Los Angeles was the first on-campus counseling program established for lesbian and gay youth in a public school. This unprecedented success at changing local school policy has also provided a new source of research and education concerning homophobia in public high schools. The New York City schools initially passed sweeping curricula changes that included recommended texts concerning lesbian and gay families in elementary schools as well as changes in high school curricula, though such changes remain the focus of renewed controversy.

Lesbian and gay educators have increasingly examined their impact on, and responsibility toward, lesbian and gay students. The book, *Coming Out of the Classroom Closet,* provides a public discussion of the seriousness with which teachers address the idea of "coming out" publicly. Teachers now consider the possibility that they can set personal examples of responsible, professional adulthood with which homosexual youth can identify. They also fear that disclosure may be viewed as unprofessional or unethical. Despite these concerns, lesbian and gay educators have addressed curricula issues that impact the self-esteem of gay and lesbian youth. Particular focus has been on fields such as psychology and family life education. Another area of concern has been the public health obligation of educators to lesbian and gay youngsters within the context of AIDS. Heterosexual and homosexual educators increasingly recognize the value of candor with students when examining homosexual themes in literature, the arts, and history.

Change still comes slowly in school settings, but there is an encouraging trend toward curricula and programs affecting lesbian and gay youth and their families. There is also increasing recognition of the need for heterosexual and homosexual youth to have accurate information about AIDS, homosexuality, and the roles of homosexuals as intellectuals, as parents and relatives, as victims of persecution and as political advocates.

School districts inclined to change homophobic policies tend to be located in cities with large, well organized lesbian and gay communities and sophisticated constituents. Strong opposition to such changes still exists, however, even in these settings. For example, the coalition effort by Pat Robertson and the local Catholic Diocese to change New York City's school curriculum succeeded in removing some recommended materials. Of course, some religious coalitions pose a powerful threat to efforts at making schools more supportive for lesbian and gay youth. The "religious right" has targeted school board elections in communities nationwide to gain strategic influence on school curricula and the nation's youth. Candidates labeled as "stealth candidates" because they withhold information about their religious and political agenda, are running increasingly successful school board campaigns in many localities. Once elected, they attempt to codify homophobia and "family values" curricula, to reinstate school prayer, and in some areas to counter the teaching of evolution by including the religious ideology of "creationism" in curricula (Conason, 1993).

The "religious right" seems to have a much larger agenda than the "family values" campaigns suggest. The "religious right" does not simply encourage homophobic fears from the past, or impede policy change on behalf of lesbian and gay youth. This interest group poses a threat to many policies and traditions in American education such as the separation of the secular school system from the church community. While homophobia is a powerful cultural influence, it is important in this policy debate that advocates for lesbian and gay youth invoke the historic traditions of pluralism in America, as well as the constitutionally mandated separation of church and state. This strategy makes it more likely that coalitions will develop with other groups impacted by the infusion of certain religious values into school policies. Whether Pat Robertson, the "religious right," and the "traditional values" coalition, even in concert with the Catholic Church, will be able, over the long run, to seriously impede efforts to reduce homophobia in the New York City public school system is uncertain, as are the long term implications of these campaigns.

Several cities nationwide provide specialized services for gay and lesbian youth. Cities like Los Angeles, New York, Boston, Washington, D.C., Chicago, and San Francisco have large gay and lesbian populations. They also have significant numbers of homeless, runaway, and pushout gay and lesbian youth. These youth pose an important challenge to homophobic policies within the school system. They become agents for change in school settings, as well as the subjects of disruption and controversy on some campuses. In order to increase their own understanding and that of others about homosexuality, many students have used Project 10 in Los Angeles, the Boston Alliance for Gay and Lesbian Youth in Boston, the Hetrick-Martin Institute in New York, Horizons in Chicago, the Sexual Minority Assistance League in Washington, D.C., the Lavender Youth Information and Recreation Center in San Francisco, and similar programs. They have also used these programs to have counseling and socializing opportunities, and to address special topics of importance to them such as AIDS (Cohen & Cohen, 1992). In New York City and Los Angeles, the school districts have also collaborated with lesbian and gay community youth serving organizations to develop separate schools for those youth who do not successfully integrate into a general student body. Sometimes, these youngsters eventually involve themselves in efforts to change the institutions they once found so alienating. Therefore, lesbian and gay youth, as well as adult youth advocates, are part of an activist constituency addressing homophobic policy in youth-serving institutions.

Homeless and runaway gay and lesbian youngsters, some as young as 13, were first noticed as fixtures in the underworld of the lesbian and gay community during the mid-1970s (Stonewall Recovery Services, 1983). These youth, often abused or neglected in their families of origin, usually survived primarily by prostitution. The newly developing visible lesbian and gay community struggled for social acceptance and respect. The children's visible presence created the opposite aura. These youngsters had chronic drug and alcohol abuse problems, as well as severe depression and self-destructive impulses. Many of them eventually contracted AIDS. Street youth belong to no one, and have nowhere to belong. They were the first clearly identifiable population of gay and lesbian children visible to the heterosexual society because of encounters with police, probation officers and social workers. They were also visible to the lesbian and gay community because of street hustling and constant loitering around lesbian and gay establishments. Though now the focus of a growing array of services, these youngsters are still the most needy and visible segment of all lesbian and gay youth.

Police, probation and social service departments learned early on that the heterosexual world had no place for these youngsters. Their families could not or would not accept them. They became chronic placement failures in group or foster care, and often were rejected outright for foster placement. They also suffered abuse by peers in school and placement settings, and while in placement, exhibited the high incidence of substance abuse, depression, suicide, dropout, runaway episodes and sexual acting out behaviors they developed in the streets.

Lesbian and gay professionals were the first to develop targeted programs for these youngsters, initially advocating for policy changes and community responses on behalf of these youngsters and eventually evolving to offer the services for which they lobbied. Despite these efforts, many of the problems initially noted among street youth persist. (See elsewhere in this volume for a discussion of some of the services and programs which have been developed for gay and lesbian youth.)

The communication between the heterosexual and the lesbian and gay communities on behalf of these youngsters ironically led to improved relations between the lesbian and gay community and key organizations in the heterosexual community, including the police. During the 1970s and early 1980s, expanding cooperation between leadership in the lesbian and gay and heterosexual communities, aimed at addressing joint concerns, occurred in Boston, New York, Los Angeles and San Francisco, with homeless youth being a common focus. Thus, a new path opened for lesbians and gays to affect social policy issues by cultivating relationships with elected officials, police, and social agencies to cooperatively address problems. These shared efforts, such as addressing the needs of lesbian and gay street youth, allowed heterosexual and homosexual professionals to interact in non-adversarial roles from a professional, rather than personal, position. This process reduced homophobia and increased mutual respect.

Efforts on behalf of lesbian and gay street youth were among several joint efforts that became the prototype for a new form of activism. Through cooperative efforts between community leaders and lesbian and gay activists, an increasingly diverse array of social policy and social welfare issues became a public focus of the lesbian and gay community in the late 1970s and 1980s. Lesbian and gay activists in Los Angeles used their Gay and Lesbian Community Services Center to address community problems in a public and cooperative relationship with private sector leaders and public officials. These activists became increasingly viewed as public servants who addressed problems like substance abuse, street youth, AIDS, mental illness, police community relations, hate crimes, and violence against women and children. This model of lesbian and gay activism offers an alternative face to the traditional adversarial approach of minority civil rights movements, and is still part of the tactical repertoire of the lesbian and gay movement. Often, the non-adversarial effort will be coupled with adversarial activities, such as demonstrations and civil disobedience, as a means of developing solutions to problems.

As an approach to advocacy for lesbian and gay youth, the non-adversarial model is highly effective. Joint efforts between heterosexual and lesbian and gay adults on behalf of these youngsters are found in many arenas such as mental health, youth advocacy and child welfare (Muller, 1987). Precisely because these efforts focus on the children's actual needs rather than on activist agendas, the programs developed seem to be less vulnerable to homophobic attacks. The inclusion of heterosexual as well as homosexual advocates also reduces the impact of attacks by opposing groups.

Since the needs of lesbian and gay youth are of genuine concern to many heterosexuals as well as homosexuals, shared efforts to help these youth are appropriate and effective. This approach insulates advocates from discrediting maneuvers such as labeling groups as "special interests," or services as "special rights." The inclusion of heterosexual leadership broadens the base of support for lesbian and gay youth at a time when their issues are the subject of considerable public controversy, and also serves to neutralize opposition tactics which otherwise might fragment efforts to develop responsible policy on behalf of these children. By including a broad constituency of lesbian and gay, as well as non-gay youth advocates, a focused theme for lesbian and gay youth policy can be both proposed and defended.

Certain questions are usually asked or implied when considering social policy and lesbian and gay youth. For instance, people ask, "Do these youngsters really exist?" Are they really "homosexual," or are they just exhibiting homosexual behavior that they can be coerced or encouraged to change, stop, or control? Will the behavior just disappear given the appropriate circumstance, such as maturity, marriage, counseling, or removal of "homosexual influences?" Sometimes these questions are posed for the purpose of homophobic debate, but often they are questions of genuine concern. Answers to these questions can be uncertain, especially for any individual child. At times, it may be appropriate to sidestep such questions, in order to keep the debate focused on a specific policy issue. At other times, when these questions can be addressed, community members can become more informed, and often are reassured.

The task of developing appropriate policies and services for gay and lesbian youth and their peers is complex, because knowledge about the development of sexuality is still somewhat limited. As noted earlier, most of today's adults were denied accurate, unbiased information about homosexuality in their own youth.

If youngsters self-identify as homosexual and, despite all pressures to conform, insist on this identity, then policy makers should be persuaded that a legitimate population of lesbian and gay youth exists. The next issue, from a policy perspective, is determining which services and policies the population needs. Policy debates must also consider the reactions of both lesbian and gay youth advocates and other constituents to proposed policies or services.

Of course, there have always been policies regarding homosexuals or homosexual behavior. For example, there is the military ban on homosexuals. More commonly, though, there simply is no specific policy in many institutions concerning homosexuals. Most high schools don't have policies against same sex couples attending school dances. However, if a student senate or school board enacts a policy stating that same sex couples can't be barred from such events, the policy makers can expect a reaction from constituents. Any attempt to change a ban that has been formalized in the past, such as the military ban, is usually even more difficult, since ending a stated policy changes the status quo, whereas creating a new policy merely formalizes a new or existing position.

Efforts to develop services for a given population such as counseling for lesbian and gay youth or housing for street youth, is likely to be somewhat easier than creating or rescinding overall policy. Services can often be established upon demonstration of the need and the existence of resources to meet the need. If the service is consistent with the purpose and goals of the organization being lobbied, then the service can be readily instituted. If not, organizational policy would need to change, which might impede the effort to establish the service. Sometimes advocates choose a lesbian and gay organization at which to establish a service, rather than try to change policies within an organization that might be resistant. This approach can, however, lead to ghettoization of service delivery.

Advocates for lesbian and gay youth initially challenged policy makers in an arena where they were sure to meet little opposition. Lesbian and gay street youth had no other advocates, and were seen as a disruptive element within agencies whose mission is to serve troubled youth. Therefore, those serving street youth have seldom confronted the forces of a Dan Quayle or a Pat Robertson when advocating for, or offering services to, lesbian and gay street youth. Rather than finding opposition, lesbian and gay youth advocates in this arena discovered that traditional youth agencies needed to find an enclave that could absorb these children in exile. There have been limited organized efforts to disrupt the services offered to lesbian and gay street youth by lesbian and gay agencies, although there have been sporadic efforts to introduce legislation in Congress which would prohibit federal funds being awarded to agencies "advocating a gay lifestyle" (Today Show, NBC, 1991). Though apparently not by design, lesbian and gay youth advocates seem to have met the least resistance simply by focusing on the most visible and pressing service need of lesbian and gay youth.

By beginning at the most accessible group of lesbian and gay youth, the first lesbian and gay youth advocates were motivated by essentially humanitarian instincts, and were not establishing a strategy for helping all lesbian and gay youth. Rather, these advocates decided to assist lesbian and gay street youth because traditional agencies could not effectively offer these services. Fortunately for the youth, the agencies charged with providing services were willing to accept assistance from the lesbian and gay community. Certain lesbian and gay youth, particularly homeless youth, seem to require their own complement of services, often including schools, that are separate from mainstream institutions.

Most gay youngsters, however, remain in mainstream settings. They are often harassed and even sometimes physically attacked in these school settings. Many underachieve or leave school, develop alcohol or drug problems, or contemplate suicide. Programs such as Project 10 in Los Angeles offer support groups for lesbian and gay youth in public high schools, but these programs have yet to bring severe hazing and ostracism under sufficient control so as to insure safety for large numbers of lesbian and gay students. With the spread of AIDS, these children are in greater peril and present even more complex social service needs than before (AIDS Surveillance Reports, 1991 and 1993).

The development of services for lesbian and gay youth parallels the development of the adult homosexual community in many ways. Advocates for lesbian and gay youth have established nearly a full complement of "separate but equal programs" while continuing to advocate for greater responsiveness to, integration opportunities for, and recognition of lesbian and gay youth on the part of mainstream youth serving organizations and policy makers. As noted earlier, in many cases, it was simpler to develop services for youth in lesbian and gay settings than it would have been to change mainstream organizations. Traditional agencies will often support creation of separate services for these youth more readily than they will change their programs to integrate these youth. In addition, lesbian and gay community members and professionals have responded more readily than their heterosexual counterparts in developing a support base for these children.

The need for advocacy on behalf of lesbian and gay youth continues to be critical. Studies regarding hazing and physical assaults of sexual minority youth in public high schools, private liberal arts colleges and the military indicate that gays and lesbians under 22 years of age are at very high risk of being victimized, even in settings usually considered accepting of diversity (Norris, 1992). The need of young people who may be presumed to be homosexual, or who are openly lesbian or gay, for protection from such harassment in mainstream settings cannot be overstated. This issue may pose policy questions related to free speech and free association, however, incidents of hazing and assault point to the heart of the question of equal protection.

In elementary and high schools, where attendance is compulsory, the need to insure a safe setting for all students, including homosexual youth, is especially compelling. Safety at school has become a grave problem for all students with the increasing presence of weapons and gangs on many campuses. The safety of lesbian and gay students, especially protection from hazing, has always been a serious problem, but as campus violence increases, so do the dangers for lesbian and gay students. Along with the need for AIDS education and prevention services, hazing and assaults on school campuses seem to be among the most critical policy issues affecting lesbian and gay youngsters.

Both the New York and Los Angeles public school systems have enacted policies and curricula changes to reduce homophobia in schools, and to provide additional support to lesbian and gay youth. Project 10 began on a single campus located near a heavily lesbian and gay neighborhood and has been expanded district-wide. New York City schools introduced a formal curriculum for all grade levels that includes stories and educational information about lesbian and gay families. The curricula has become the focus of hotly contested school board policy debates, as a result of which some elementary texts have not been adopted. Subsequently, these programs were targeted by a Pat Robertson/Catholic Diocese coalition, aimed at rescinding the non-homophobic curricula.

Less formally, many educators have included curricula regarding gay and lesbian issues, and have presented speakers on the topic in high school and college classrooms nationwide for years. Homosexual content has increased in high school and college courses covering homosexual themes in literature and art; biographical information about famous people who were homosexual or bisexual; the AIDS crisis and the responses to it; research into psychobiology and sexual development; minority civil rights movements; and family life education. Some of these areas of study have been formalized into standardized curricula where community support makes this possible. In other districts, individual teachers include such material in classroom discussion, lectures, or readings, without benefit of official sanction or policy changes.

Whether formalized or not, discussion of matters related to homosexuality within a non-homophobic context is an important tool through which to positively impact the lives of gay and lesbian youth. As overt and sanctioned homophobia decreases, so do incidents of harassment (Akin and Gallagher, 1993; Levine, 1993). Tolerant inclusion of gay and lesbian issues in the classroom also serves to validate not only the gay or lesbian youngster, but also those students who are relatives of gay or lesbian adults. Such inclusion reduces the pervasive feelings of isolation which these youngsters often report (Rench, 1990). Policy makers in many areas fear the repercussions of officially endorsing the use of curricula that include homosexual issues, but will tolerate curricula changes which occur at less formal levels.

Another policy issue is that of ending codified discrimination in agencies that serve large numbers of youth. Most theorists believe that sexual identity is formed in early childhood, however, conscious awareness of a lesbian or gay identity is often delayed until late adolescence or early adulthood. For this reason, organizations that have young constituents and that officially ban open homosexuality, such as the U.S. military, routinely admit men and women at age 18 as heterosexual who by 19 are, or wish to be, actively lesbian or gay. For this and other reasons, the intense debate regarding the U.S. military ban on gays very likely impacts a disproportionate number of lesbian and gay youth who chose military service before they consciously realized their sexual identity. In *Conduct Unbecoming*, Shilts (1993) has indicated that, while in military service, this age group has been particularly victimized by interrogation and harassment, not to mention outright assault. Thompson (1993) made similar observations when a group of Marines were acquitted on charges that they assaulted a gay man.

Not only do policies banning open homosexuals from military service or from other organizations raise important civil rights questions, they also raise serious practical questions, especially when applied to youthful populations. Lesbians and gays are virtually indistinguishable from their peers, and are therefore difficult to identify and expel. In addition, lesbian and gay youth are in a complicated developmental phase that may prevent them and anyone else from knowing when homosexuality will become an important issue for them. In trying to manage such a population by banning it, policy makers are chasing phantoms. Furthermore, investigations that take on the quality of "witch hunts" only serve to damage morale and the credibility of those conducting such activities.

Like the military, college campuses also serve the 18- to 22-year-old population. As early as 1970, small groups of lesbian and gay students began forming student organizations. These groups, like most student groups, sponsored conferences, social events and speakers. They also lobbied for changes in university policy and curricula, changes in policies in other student organizations, and changes in larger institutional and community policy arenas. On many large campuses, these groups have evolved into student centers for lesbian and gay students, and have helped to make substantial changes in university policy (Malkin, 1993). Some policy changes have resulted in the inclusion of lesbian and gay couples in married student housing, allocation of student body funds for lesbian and gay events, and protection of lesbian and gay students from hazing. In addition, significant inclusion of homosexual issues has occurred in both teaching and research as a consequence of these efforts.

These improvements in student life for lesbians and gays is of considerable importance to the whole intellectual community and, by its influence, to the entire society. Ironically, it was lesbian and gay youth, a population whose very existence remains mired in controversy and denial, who developed small student organizations for friendship and support that have evolved into a substantial force vis á vis university life, research, and curricula. Lesbian and gay intellectuals, and their themes, have always been important to the intellectual community. At least in part, credit for more openness is due to lesbian and gay youth, who came of age and took action on their own behalf during the past 20 years. The success of these groups testifies to the importance of ongoing activism by lesbian and gay youth in the university setting, if understanding of homosexuality, documentation of the intellectual contributions of lesbians and gays, and future research efforts in homosexuality and related fields are to continue (Ansen & Foote, 1993).

Despite such apparent acceptance of homosexuality and homosexuals on college campuses today, hazing and harassment of lesbian and gay students in these settings is a continuing problem. Most campuses have ordinances against hazing, but efforts to use policy to enforce the concept of the safe educational environment have been challenged as violations of the First Amendment. As a case in point, after extensive efforts to suppress racist and sexist harassment, the University of Wisconsin acknowledged that these behaviors couldn't really be managed at the policy level (Siegel, 1993). Similar controversies have brewed over efforts to address racism by regulating expression at Wellesley College, and at the University of Pennsylvania (News Release, ABC News, 1993). Reports from other 'liberal-minded' institutions, such as Oberlin College, indicate that harassment of sexual minorities also continues at a significant level.

Many campus conflicts, and some courtroom battles in the 1980s, concerned national policy issues, such as Affirmative Action. There were also serious conflicts over curriculum content, and over new concepts related to diversity within the intellectual setting, as reflected in the content of courses concerning "Cultural Relativism." These matters have been of concern to the intellectual community, and to minority faculty and students, especially to lesbians and gays of color. However, the efforts to modify course content to reflect new ideas regarding culture, gender, race, ethnicity, and sexuality have often become ensnared in political, rather than intellectual concerns (Harvard Magazine, 1993).

Lesbian and gay students have concerns in addition to their basic concern as a minority population. Lesbian and gay students, faculty and supporters will press for policies that provide for curricula changes to include homosexual issues and non-homophobic concepts, opportunities for research into homosexual-related concerns, and increased research related to AIDS. Lesbian and gay students and their non-gay supporters will also continue to press for greater access to all services and programs within the university through efforts to end discrimination in housing, insurance, student health programs, fraternities and sororities, and student activities that exclude either lesbians and gays, or their partners and children. For instance, considerable pressure has been placed on campuses that have ROTC programs in light of U.S. military policy excluding lesbian and gay ROTC students.

Efforts to curb hazing and harassment of students on campus may need several different policy approaches. One approach might focus on strengthening the sense of community among all students, rather than focusing on sanctions aimed toward undesirable behavior. For instance, instituting new programs on campus that are designed to increase respect and understanding among diverse student bodies, including homosexual students, might be helpful. Students might also benefit from workshops designed to help them resolve conflicts and disputes in less adversarial ways. Universities might offer programs for direct on-campus mediation of student disputes as well as arbitration of disputes, and may decide to assist individual students in developing their negotiation and dispute resolution skills. Often, such programs outdistance both policy statements and sanctions in discouraging bigotry.

Behaviors that threaten free speech and free association within the community, and behaviors that threaten the safety of community members call for sanctions. Those advocating for lesbian and gay youth must participate with policy makers and other minority youth advocates, especially in school and college settings, to develop policies that insure free speech and also protect students from hazing, physical assault, and harassment.

Lesbian and gay youth, like other youngsters, belong to churches, social clubs and recreational groups. These organizations vary widely in terms of policies regarding gay and lesbian youth. Some churches and temples have educational programs that encourage tolerance and understanding. In these settings, lesbian and gay youth may be afraid of having family or friends know that they are homosexual, but they probably feel some tacit acceptance and experience less damaged self-concepts than do lesbian and gay children in religious groups that actively condemn homosexuality. Youth-serving organizations, such as the Boy Scouts of America, often seem to lag behind schools in their efforts to address the concerns of lesbian and gay youth. With the exception of the Boy Scouts, activists have not challenged policies in youth serving organizations to any great degree.

Youth leadership, especially, needs to be professionally trained regarding lesbian and gay youth. Gay and lesbian youngsters may be harassed by peers or may seek guidance from leaders about matters they are unable to discuss with their parents. Assuring troubled teens a place to talk with an understanding adult could help lower the rate of depression for lesbian and gay youth. The pressing need of lesbian and gay youth for social support and access to counseling is likely to motivate increased efforts to reduce homophobia in youth group settings.

Successful challenges to homophobic policy, even through the courts, tend to have certain characteristics. There must be a dedicated constituency requesting the change, who are connected to, and supported by, the larger lesbian and gay community. Support from heterosexuals, including organizations like Parents and Friends of Lesbians and Gays, or the National Education Association is important. Successful challenges often involve influential leaders, who impact organizations either from within, or by exerting pressure from the larger community. Effective advocates for change generally formulate a clear, specific agenda, and have a plan by which to achieve this agenda. Successful lesbian and gay advocates use well developed, persuasive arguments regarding the pressing need for change, which describe benefits to the constituents affected, and which refute opposing arguments. There must also be the component of commitment, as there will be many, well organized, well financed, and equally committed opponents. Homophobia is a deeply ingrained value, fueled by profound fears regarding the need to protect youth from homosexuals.

Mainstream youth organizations are usually run by parents who are very involved with their children. Youthful members of these groups, though some are certainly gay and need support, are not abandoned street youth. They are members of ordinary families, whose parents intend to protect their children and their children's organization from influences of which they disapprove. These parents are motivated to resist any policy change regarding homosexuality. They intend to raise their children to be heterosexual, and expect organizations like the Boy Scouts of America to help them do so.

Motivation with its origin in personal experience can bring enormous energy for social change, and can also bring resistance to social change. Many gay and lesbian social change activists had been in foster care as youth, or had been rejected by their families. Undoubtedly, some of the energy they expended to reform the child welfare system and to develop programs for lesbian and gay street youth came from an intrinsic, internal source. In addition to other motives, they may have identified with those abandoned lesbian and gay children who found themselves at the mercy of the child welfare system. Thus, they may have been more deeply moved to embrace these youth. Since both those who advocate for, and those who resist change, can have deep personal motivations, these feelings can fuel long, hard-fought struggles over social policy issues.

The sustained commitment to change social policy in this area may, indeed, *require* an intrinsic motivation born of one's own suffering, the suffering or needs of one's own children, or that of other friends and family. To the extent that such intrinsic motivation is present, the energy to struggle continues. As a result of that sustained commitment, organizations like the Boy Scouts and the U.S. military will be continually and repeatedly challenged to change. Likewise, schools and universities will also be challenged to reduce homophobia in these settings.

Both the proponents and opponents of non-homophobic policy have already demonstrated a nearly 20 year commitment to their cause. Thus, each side already has a great personal investment of time and energy added to the initial motives which press them onward. Lesbian and gay activists also show a deeper resolve to improve the lives of lesbian and gay youth as well as lesbian and gay families in the wake of AIDS. These strong intrinsic motivations on each side suggest that the policy debates concerning lesbian and gay youth will continue for some time.

Lesbian and gay youngsters under the age of 18 are children, both in the eyes of the law, and in terms of social policy. As such, unless abandoned or in the custody of authorities, their parents, usually heterosexual, have the moral and legal right and responsibility to decide the health, education and religious lifestyles of their children. There has, however, been increasing opportunity to seek legal redress on their own behalf when their interests conflict with their parents' interests, especially for older children.

Child advocacy groups, such as the Child Welfare League of America and the Children's Defense Fund, made significant gains for children in the arena of social policy during the 1970s and 1980s, in the areas of child abuse reporting and investigation procedures, foster care programs, domestic violence services, child custody dispute resolution programs, and child and family therapy services (Bozett and Sussman, 1990). However, serious losses occurred in other child-policy areas, such as funding for education and health care for children (Sosin and Caulum, 1983). These changes affected lesbian and gay youth as well.

Changes which empower children, such as changes in child abuse laws, foster care, and legal rights for children especially impact lesbian and gay youth. Lesbian and gay youth are at risk for significant conflict with their parents, especially as the sexual identity of these children likely becomes evident during adolescence. Parents may bring enormous, even abusive, pressure on lesbian and gay children, in order to thwart homosexual impulses or nontraditional gender role behaviors (Margh, 1993). Clearly defined and enforced child abuse laws should protect lesbian and gay children from such abuses of parental power.

Related gains in child therapy, family therapy, AIDS treatment and prevention, suicide prevention for youth, and substance abuse treatment and prevention programs all address specific health and mental health problems which may disproportionately affect lesbian and gay youth (Suggs, 1993). Efforts within the health professions to reduce homophobia among pediatric and family practice professionals will have a salutary impact on lesbian and gay youth.

Arguably the most important policy change in mental health since 1970, was the depathologizing of homosexuality, as a result of which homosexuality was removed from the list of diagnostic categories recognized by the American Psychiatric Association (Gitterman and Miller, 1989). That change brought forth a shift in clinical approaches to treating depression, anxiety, and all other mental health problems among lesbians and gays. The change at the APA was followed by changes in research and teaching curricula at schools of social work, psychology and medicine. Curricula were redesigned to sensitize practitioners to the need for nonhomophobic treatment for lesbians and gays and methods by which lesbians and gays can achieve positive self-identities. In this instance, advocacy at the national level changed policy in a key profession which prompted change at many levels of teaching, research and practice in that and related professions. This policy change came from the top downward and has helped huge numbers of lesbian and gay youth as well as adults. Other policy changes with key implications, as in the case of Project 10, have come upward from the classroom level to the Board of Education.

In the arena of mental health care, practitioners seek to identify the need for, and the impact of, healthy lesbian and gay role models in these children's lives. Some practitioners recommend that lesbian and gay therapists can best treat these youngsters due to their greater knowledge of the socialization and stigmatization issues involved. Many practitioners also note the dangers of unconscious homophobia on the part of heterosexual providers serving lesbian and gay youth. Policy makers in clinics, hospitals, training institutes and funding sources, such as the National Institutes of Health increasingly grapple with advocates who suggest that specialized training, services, programs and personnel are needed to serve lesbian and gay youth. Consequently, more funding has become available for research and treatment in these areas.

Some issues are of immediate and critical concern in the areas of health and mental health services for lesbian and gay youth. AIDS is the foremost concern. Lesbian and gay youth must have the full complement of AIDS prevention and treatment services. The rate of HIV infection in the U.S. has grown over time, and the growth rate of AIDS cases among gay male teens is among the fastest.

Furthermore, it can be reasonably inferred that conversion to sero-positive status or a diagnosis of AIDS by the early 20s evidences HIV infection during the teenage years. For this reason, if no other, appropriate AIDS prevention services are needed for all teenagers, especially gay teens. During the mid and late 1980s, increasing pressure was put on policy makers to address the needs of teens at high risk for HIV exposure and AIDS. An effort by the Rand Corporation to identify these youngsters in a survey of sexual behavior among teens met enormous resistance (Rand Corporation news releases, 1991, 1993). For clearly political reasons, the data collection shifted from a survey of all students to a survey of students whose parents permitted participation. This shift created skewed sampling. The homophobic quality of the debate obscured other methodological issues, including data collection and the quality of self-reports of sexual behavior by teens. Denial of the presence of lesbian and gay youth, homophobia, and misinformation fueled the resistance to defining and quantifying homosexual behavior among youth. Spokespeople for the resistance consisted mainly of legislators supported by the so-called "religious right." Those objecting to the study expressed fears that surveying young men about their sexual behavior with, or sexual interest in, same sex partners would possibly induce such feelings, or offer permission for such feelings, and thus encourage homosexual behavior.

These spokespeople have support from a well organized constituency of voters, motivated by religious zeal to oppose all measures even remotely supportive of homosexual concerns. These groups are particularly reactive to matters concerning youth. The homophobic agenda of the "religious right" extends beyond concerns about minors (Duffy, 1992; Conason, 1993). While initially characterizing AIDS as a "gay disease," some of these groups express the belief that those with AIDS are being punished by God for their prior misconduct, and thus have opposed public funding of AIDS related services and research on such grounds. Efforts to address the concerns of lesbian and gay youth with respect to AIDS can be expected to produce considerable resistance from these groups, though, remarkably, there have not been significant challenges from the right to efforts to assist lesbian and gay street youth even when the help is offered by adult lesbians and gays. Rather, their focus has been on the perceived possible homosexual influence on those youngsters who are not among those youth classified as street youth.

The motives and support base of the anti-homosexual activists need to be systematically understood by lesbian and gay youth advocates. The influence of anti-homosexual groups on social policy in America seems to have grown, despite losses of some battles, even the loss of their candidate of choice in the 1992 presidential election (TIME Magazine, 1992; Postrel, 1993). Advocates for lesbian and gay youth must know the opposition, and understand its tactics and strategies. Additional knowledge will help advocates to forge more effective coalitions and tactics of their own to counter the influence of anti-homosexual activists. These groups have spent considerable time and money studying the lesbian and gay movement, and have funded their own think tanks. If lesbian and gay activists can anticipate upcoming anti-homosexual strategies and campaigns, then these strategies and campaigns can be neutralized more effectively. The election of Bill Clinton as President will likely have an empowering effect on the overall direction of the gay and lesbian civil rights movement. It appears that extremist positions taken by certain spokespersons for the religious right at the Republican National Convention in 1992, with respect to the "threat" that gays and lesbians pose to the moral fabric of America, moved potential voters away from the Republican Presidential ticket.

Partly as the result of newly formed coalitions with other minority groups, policy debates in the future will likely expand the areas of change that occurred during the 1980s. These areas principally have focused on lesbian and gay youth above age 13. For youth above age 18, policy debates will likely continue to be focused in the institutions where they are most concentrated such as universities, colleges, and the military, and will continue to involve the youth themselves.

Within organizations serving 13- to 18-year-olds, policy changes will likely occur because of pressure from advocates, and also from the youth themselves. Changes can be expected in curricula, in nondiscrimination efforts, and in continued development of specialized programs for homosexuals that range from student centers to counseling groups. Increased support from understanding parents, from lesbian and gay youth service advocates, and from general youth advocacy groups can be expected to continue to increase. Specialized services for 13- to 18-year-old street youth, institutionalized youth, and abandoned and abused youth will likely expand over time, as will specialized services for children and youth who have HIV or AIDS. Agencies serving street youth will continue to be very active, and will expand services for gay and lesbian youth.

Similar youth-serving programs and agencies will develop in many communities, both urban and rural, and will offer mixtures of residential and nonresidential services for these youth. The development and survival of such agencies will depend on funding availability, and on the priorities of local lesbian and gay communities as well as on the policy-based priorities of local city, county, and state agencies. Support from parent groups, and from the children of lesbians and gays will continue to be an important force for changing youth policy as regards lesbian and gay youth.

The lesbian and gay community, despite the significant loss of leadership and experience as the result of AIDS, has continued its development as a force for social change. Even as acceptance increases, young gays and lesbians will still need the support of their community. In this framework, lesbians and gays must identify needs which their own organizations must continue to meet, and issues around which to seek social change. The needs of lesbian and gay youth will continue to be among those concerns.

Family issues, indeed the definition of family, will also be an ongoing concern affecting lesbian and gay youth as lesbian and gay families mature. Modern technology, especially biomedical technology, opened a new world of lifestyle options for lesbians and gays during the 1980s and 1990s. The advent of easily accessible artificial insemination and in vitro fertilization techniques provided new options in child bearing to gays and lesbians. Increasing numbers of lesbian and gay couples are raising their own children. Greater numbers of lesbian and gay couples are foster and adoptive parents as well. These technological changes, along with changes in social attitudes, redefined the "family unit" during the 1980s. The existence of these new family constellations has opened a new set of policy issues. It may, eventually, even become necessary for members of the religious right to develop policies that help all families and children cope, rather than seeking to develop policies that promote or define particular types of families.

These changes profoundly affect lesbian and gay children and youth. As parents, lesbian and gay adults will likely be more concerned about, and involved in, efforts to reduce homophobia in schools and organizations serving children. They will be a source of support and influence when lesbian and gay youth advocates try to end discrimination, change curricula and texts, and institute counseling or other special services for lesbian and gay youth.

The future impact of science and technology on policies regarding lesbian and gay youth will likely become increasingly significant. Often, parents believe that homosexuality can be thwarted by encouraging, or even forcing, children to adhere to rigid gender roles. Such efforts have not effectively impeded homosexual development in earlier generations, but rather have been the source of abuse of lesbian and gay youth.

As research further clarifies the nature of homosexual development and the development of human sexuality itself, policy decisions can address the implications of such research. Even as inferences are drawn and new policy challenges developed, there will be policy debates regarding the validity and even the continuance of such research. For many, the idea that homosexuality may occur under biologic influence within the natural order of human sexuality is unacceptable. As new information regarding homosexuality and biology emerges, however, it appears that the homosexual impulse is present from birth. This impulse may lie quiescent through early childhood and latency, and emerge in adolescence. Or the impulse may be expressed in another form, such as nontraditional gender role identification, or androgyny. Or, that which we call homosexual identity now, may prove to be part of a conglomerate of qualities, of which lesbian and gay orientations are a part.

When linked to research on gender and brain development, the implications of new ideas concerning gender, sexuality, and mental development lead to more connections between gender, sexuality, and intellectual pursuits than had been previously thought. Nature, or the hereditary factor, appears to be a significant influence, along with environment, in the development of sexual orientation. It would be premature to predict how these scientific developments will shape policy, especially for lesbian and gay youngsters, but it is certain that the influence of such new ideas will be part of future policy controversies concerning youth.

There is no evidence that exposure of children to homosexual adults predisposes them toward homosexuality. Studies of homosexual couples as parents indicate that homosexual couples and heterosexual couples are about equally likely to rear heterosexual children, though lesbian couples show slightly greater, though statistically insignificant, likelihood of rearing heterosexual children than do heterosexual couples or gay male couples in these studies. There do seem to be some possible predisposing genetic factors for homosexuality, as shown in twin studies of both lesbians and gay men, as well as in some family studies. There may be some factors related to prenatal conditions which are also predisposing influences for homosexuality. Other effects on homosexual development such as particular parenting styles, have not yet been as clearly implicated.

Future policy ramifications of these studies for lesbian and gay youngsters are not yet clear, in part because the data are new and still only suggestive. These data repeatedly argue against any possibility that lesbian and gay adults influence the sexuality of youngsters. To the extent that confirming data continue to suggest biologic determinants of homosexuality, there will likely be greater pressure on youth-serving institutions to respond to the needs of, to provide protection for gay and lesbian youth, and to change homophobic curricula and policies.

Improving the knowledge base of teachers and counselors about homosexuality, and using parent education to expose the dangers for lesbian and gay youngsters of homophobic child rearing practices, seem to be key tasks in future policy change efforts. Advocates and policy makers may need to more readily and comfortably assume that there are now children who, as adolescents or adults, will be homosexual. As the population is acknowledged, advocates can propose policies and programs to help lesbian and gay youth become fully developed and self-determining human beings. While many professional organizations and schools, including the National Association of Social Workers and the American Medical Association, have officially denounced homophobic attitudes, these groups must advocate more directly and aggressively for increased programs for these children and their families (Gummer, 1988; Silverman and Silverman, 1986).

The homosexual community has revealed itself to be an heroic element in American society, as evidenced by its responses to AIDS. *Newsweek* surveyed the losses to the arts due to the AIDS epidemic, noting that a generation of writers, visual artists, performers, directors and choreographers has been lost at its prime (Ansen et al., 1993). A significant proportion of these people were gay or bisexual and, perhaps for the first time, the larger population was able to glimpse the loss to its own quality of life brought by the loss of these gay men. It is now clear that large numbers of homosexuals make significant contributions to society.

Policy makers have been urged to deny services, sometimes even life giving services, to homosexuals. Such anti-gay advocacy appears to be partly based on the notion that, if homosexuals are denied employment and housing, if harassment and hate crimes go unchecked, if AIDS funding is denied, and if lesbian and gay youngsters are coerced into heterosexual lives, homosexuality will disappear. The more likely scenario is that, in future years, children who will be lesbian or gay will be more readily identified at earlier life stages. The fate of such children will be a central policy question, as the nation's response to AIDS became a central policy question in the 1980s.

What will be our policies regarding lesbian and gay youth? Would heterosexual parents knowingly bring a child into the world who they knew would be lesbian or gay, if they had the choice? Should they have that choice? If a "gay gene" is actually identified, should science again focus on the effort to change the predisposition to homosexuality? Ought this trait be eradicated, if possible? These may be the future policy questions regarding lesbian and gay youth and their families.

These questions focus the theme of homophobia, and the agenda of the homophobic activists. Is eradication of homosexuality the goal? If even a possibility, could such policies lead to a world with no Dag Hammarskjold, no Tennessee Williams, James Baldwin, or Bessie Smith? To eliminate the common homosexual may be to eliminate the homosexual giant, as well. To fail to respond to the needs of lesbian and gay youth may equate to a policy that discourages the development, even the existence of such great persons, as well as neglects the millions of average homosexuals who live productive lives, surrounded by loving families and friends.

Policies which damage the self-concept of any population of youngsters, especially those that increase suicidality or substance abuse, are, by definition, flawed. Lesbian and gay youth, and the children of gay or lesbian parents, ought not to be pawns in an ideological or cultural war. They are children who are deeply affected by policies and debates regarding homosexuality.

When "protecting" children from lesbian and gay role models, when debasing lesbian and gay parents, or when attempting to coerce children into heterosexuality, few advocates of homophobic policy consider who lesbian and gay people really are. Few such policy advocates consider the positive attributes of the lesbian and gay community or how much the lesbian and gay population, even in the face of scourge and stigma, has contributed to society.

The more effectively lesbian and gay advocates and their heterosexual friends and family drive home the theme of lesbian and gay contribution to society, the more likely it is that this theme will be reflected in enlightened policy. Therefore, organizations such as Parents and Friends of Lesbians and Gays, and other groups focused on combatting bigotry and expanding civil rights, are of crucial importance to the future of lesbian and gay youth and to the development of enlightened policy. The sooner enlightened policies are developed, the sooner these youngsters will be able to lead healthier, happier, better adjusted, and more productive lives.

REFERENCES

Akin, S. & Gallagher, J. (1993). Class struggle. *The Advocate, 624,* 44-45.

Ansen, D. & Foote, D. (1993). A decade of loss: Artists who died of AIDS. *Newsweek, 121,* 22.

Austin, M. & Hershey, W., (eds.) (1982). *Handbook on mental health administration.* San Francisco: Jossey-Bass, 1982.

Bell, A. & Weinberg, M. (1978). *Homosexualities: A study of diversity among men and women.* New York: Simon & Schuster.

Berzon, B. (ed.) (1992). *Positively gay.* Berkeley: Celestial Arts.

Boxall, B. & Gerstenzang, J. (1993, April 25). Festive air reigns on eve of gay march. *Los Angeles Times,* A1, A32.

Bozett, F. & Sussman, M. (1990). *Homosexuality and family relations.* New York: Harrington Park Press.

Burr, C. (1993). Homosexuality and biology. *The Atlantic Monthly, 271(3),* 47-65.

Casey, C. (1993, March 29). Conduct unbecoming: In defense of gays on the front line. *Los Angeles Times,* E3.

Clark, D. (1987). *The new loving someone gay.* Berkeley, CA: Celestial Arts.

Cohen, S. & Cohen, D. (1992). *When someone you know is gay: High school help line.* New York: Laurel Leaf Books.

Conason, J. (1993). With God as their co-pilot: The Christian Right and U.S. politics. *Playboy, 40,* 91.

DaFoe-Whitehead, B. (1993). Dan Quayle was right. *The Atlantic Monthly 27(4),* 47-84.

DeCrescenzo, T. (1993). GLASS celebrates ninth year. *Off the Streets, GLASS Newsletter, 4,* 1.

Duffy, M. (1992). Divided they fall. *Time, 20,* 65-66.

Editorial staff of John Harvard's Journal. (1993). Ethnic studies. *Harvard Magazine, 95(5),* 71.

Fricke, A. & Fricke, W. (1991). *Sudden strangers: The story of a gay son and his father.* New York: St. Martins Press.

Friends of Project 10; *Project 10 Handbook;* Los Angeles; 1991.

Gallagher, J. (1992). The cause of sexuality is all in your head, say two UCLA biologists. *The Advocate, 611,* 19.

Gitterman, A. & Miller, I. (1989). The influence of the organization on clinical practice. *Clinical Social Work Journal, 17,* 151-164.

Goffman, E. (1963). *Stigma: Notes on the management of a spoiled identity.* Englewood Cliffs, NJ: Prentice-Hall.

Gummer, B. (1988). Management in the public sector: Privatization, policy deadlock, and the erosion of public authority. *Administration in Social Work, 12(4),* 103-118.

Harbeck, K. (1992). *Coming out of the classroom closet.* New York: Harrington Park Press.

Herdt, G. (1989). *Gay and lesbian youth.* New York: Harrington Park Press.

Hiratsuka, J. (1993). Outsiders: gay teens, straight world. *NASW News, 38(4),* 3.

The Honorable Donna Hitchens Family Court Services Statewide Training Institute. (1991, November). *Sexual preference: family relationships, legal issues, and implications for child custody and visitation.*

Hooker, E. (1963). The adjustment of the male overt homosexual. In Ruibenheek (Ed.), *The problem of homosexuality in modern society.* New York: Dutton.

Kaus, M. (1993). The godmother, Marian Wright Edelman: The Clintons' eminence grise. *The New Republic,* (208) 7, 21-25.

Kinsey, A., Pomeroy, W. & Martin, C. (1948). *Sexual behavior in the human male.* Philadelphia: Saunders.

Krauthammer, C. (1993, May 2). A parent's right to shape a child. *Los Angeles Times*, M5.

Lacayo, R. (1992). Jack and jack and jill and jill. *Time, 24*, 52-53.

Letters to the editor. (1993, August 22). *Los Angeles Times Magazine*.

Levine, B. (1993, March 9). Spelling out why gays in uniform live in fear. *Los Angeles Times*, E1-E2.

Levine, M. (1981). *The history and politics of community mental health*. New York: Oxford University Press.

Licata, S. & Petersen, R. (1985). *The gay past*. New York: Harrington Park Press.

Los Angeles County Department of Health Services. (1991, 1993). *AIDS Surveillance Reports*.

Malkin, M. (1993). Colin Powell invite by Harvard cause for anger among students. *Bay Windows, 11(16)*, 1,4.

Marcus, E. (1992). *Making history: The struggle for gay and lesbian equal rights*. New York: Harper Collins.

Maugh, T. (1993, March 12). Genetic component found in lesbianism, study says. *Los Angeles Times*, A1, A26-27.

Muller, A. (1987). *Parents matter*. Tallahassee, FL: The Naiad Press.

Muther, C. (1993). Fighting the right: A Sudbury mother battles against anti-gay school system initiatives. *Bay Windows, (11)*16.

National Center for Lesbian Rights. (1992). *The Boy Scout Bigotry: Fighting Back. A Resource Packet*. San Francisco, CA.

News Release re RAND Corporation Survey of Teen Sexual Behaviors; Today Show; NBC; Spring 1991.

News Release re RAND Corporation Survey of Teen Sexual Behaviors; National Public Radio; Spring 1993.

News Release re Racism and Free Speech at Wellesley and the University of Pennsylvania; This Week with David Brinkley; ABC News; May 2,1993.

Norris, W. (1992). Liberal attitudes and homophobic acts: The paradoxes of homosexual experience in the liberal institution. *Journal of Homosexuality, 23*, chapt. 3-4, pp. 81-121.

Pattullo, E. (1993). Why not gays in the military? *National Review, 45(4)*, 38-41.

Postrel, V. (1993). Lost causes: Diminished clout of the Republican Party's Christian Right. *Reason, 24*, 4.

Reiss-Davis Child Study Center (1993). Brochure: *Issues in working with gay and lesbian youth and families*.

Rench, J. (1990). *Understanding sexual identity: A book for gay and lesbian teens and their friends*. Minneapolis, MN: Lerner Publications Co.

Ricketts, W. & Achtenberg, R. (1990). *Adoption and foster parenting for lesbians and gay men: Creating new traditions in family*. Hazleton, PA: The Haworth Press, Inc.

Shilts, R. (1993). *Conduct unbecoming*. New York: St. Martin's Press.

Siegel, B. (1993, March 28) Speak no evil: How the University of Wisconsin tried to outlaw hate. *Los Angeles Times Magazine*, 14-20, 44-48.

Silverman, W. & Silverman, M. (1986). Staffing and organizational models in mental health programs. *Administration and Mental Health, 14*(2), 78-96.

Sosin, M. & Caulum, S. (1983). Advocacy: A conceptualization for social work practice. *Social Work, (28)*1, 12-17.

Stonewall Recovery Services. (1983). Drug/alcohol abuse prevention grants available. *Seattle Gay News, (21)*17, 14.

Suggs, D. (1993). GLAAD tidings: Goodhousekeeping. *Seattle Gay News, (21)*17, 9.

Thompson, E. (1993). Marines Acquitted in North Carolina Assault. *Bay Windows, (11)*16, 1,11.

Time Editorial Staff. (1992). Political exorcism: GOP Centrists organize to wrest the party pack from the Religious Right. *Time.*

Wofford, J. & Hamer, D. (1993). Benefits for domestic partners. *Harvard Magazine Letters, 95*(5), 122.

Counseling Strategies with Gay and Lesbian Youth

Gerald P. Mallon

SUMMARY. Counseling needs of gay and lesbian youth have not been adequately researched. Identification of these issues has only been underway for approximately ten years, as service providers and researchers turned their attention to this population. Factors which contribute to a presenting clinical picture include stigmatization, hiding and isolation, a sense of being different, lack of family support, harassment, and violence. Each of these areas is discussed, integrating case vignettes and research findings.

INTRODUCTION

By the time I was 11, I already knew I was gay and I hated myself for it. I hated myself so much that I wanted to kill myself. I wanted to be "normal." "Why me?" I'd ask myself over and over again, I even prayed to God that he or she would give me the strength to change myself. All that I ever knew about gay men at the time were the stereotypes and the lies that

Gerald P. Mallon, MSW, is Director of New York City Programs for Green Chimney Children's Services, a residential treatment center for adolescents. Mr. Mallon is completing his doctoral studies at Hunter College School of Social Work, City University of New York.

Correspondence may be directed to the author at 327 East 22nd Street, New York, NY 10010.

[Haworth co-indexing entry note]: "Counseling Strategies with Gay and Lesbian Youth." Mallon, Gerald P. Co-published simultaneously in *Journal of Gay & Lesbian Social Services* (The Haworth Press, Inc.) Vol. 1, No. 3/4, 1994, pp. 75-91; and: *Helping Gay and Lesbian Youth: New Policies, New Programs, New Practice* (ed: Teresa DeCrescenzo) The Haworth Press, Inc., 1994, pp. 75-91. Multiple copies of this article/chapter may be purchased from The Haworth Document Delivery Center [1-800-3-HAWORTH; 9:00 a.m. - 5:00 p.m. (EST)].

my parents taught me: that they were all child molesters and wanted to be women. My father was always telling me, "walk like a man, stop sitting like a woman." My parents taught me that gay people were not people at all. They taught me that they didn't deserve any respect at all. So how was I supposed to feel when I discovered that I was gay? How is someone suppose to feel when you know that your own family would never even accept you? I have heard some people say that people choose to be gay, to be honest, if I had a choice I would not have chosen to be gay. Who in the world would choose to go through all the name calling, all the bashings, and all of the other crap gay people have to go through every day?

—17 year old gay male

Lesbian and gay teenagers experience the same problems of adolescence as do other young people, but they also face additional problems unique to their situation. Their lives are often filled with struggles with which they must grapple in the context of a largely rejecting and fearful society. The difficulties which gay and lesbian teenagers face are intensified as many hide their identity from family and peers and withdraw socially because they are afraid of adverse consequences (Mallon, 1992). The experience of acquiring a homosexual identity at an early age places the young person at risk for dysfunction. Given the stigma that is attached to homosexuality in this society, adolescents who are homosexually oriented will, in some cases, have difficulty coping with stressors.

Many self-identified gay or lesbian youth cope with the stresses and tumult of the coming out process by hiding their orientation. However, hiding often leads to dysfunction, and a significant number of gay and lesbian adolescents are unable to cope with the stress. This chapter focuses on the clinical issues which are unique to the gay or lesbian adolescent; first, by examining the literature; second, by examining the various theoretical approaches which have historically been employed when dealing with homosexually oriented clients; third, by identifying clinical issues which confront the gay or lesbian adolescent; and finally, by offering suggestions to mental health care professionals who are interested in developing a more gay-affirming approach to meeting the service delivery needs of this population of young people.

Little empirical information has been collected on the gay and lesbian adolescent in need of mental health services, although the literature pertaining to gay and lesbian adults has grown. A literature search of the *Social Work Research and Abstracts* 1979-1992 revealed few articles dealing with clinical issues pertaining to gay and lesbian youth (Cates, 1987; DeCrescenzo, 1979; Hetrick & Martin, 1987; Hunter, 1990; Hunter & Schaecher, 1987, 1990; Malyon, 1981; Martin, 1982; Mercier & Berger, 1989; Needham, 1977). Schneider (1988) for the Toronto Central Youth Services and Whitlock (1989) for the American Friends Service Committee have written books on the topic. The following material is based on the author's analysis of the existing literature as well as on his clinical experience gained from working with adolescents.

THEORETICAL APPROACHES

Clinicians who work with gay, lesbian and bisexual adolescents are faced with theoretical, ethical, moral and practical decisions about how to treat those clients with same-sex orientation. Coleman (1978) notes that the illness model of homosexuality, developed by Bieber et al. (1962), focused on "curing" homosexual orientation. This theory was based on the belief that homosexuality is a result of disturbed familial relationships. Bieber posits that early childhood conflicts of an overbearing mother and a distant, absent father, and a neurotic fear of heterosexuality need to be worked out in psychoanalysis. While Bieber's work is now generally viewed by most to be theoretically unsound, it was utilized by psychoanalysts for many years. Some psychoanalysts claimed that they actually "cured" their homosexual patients (Mayerson & Lief, 1965).

Aversion, conversion and desensitization therapies have also been tried by a number of behaviorists and learning theorists (Cautela, 1967; Feldman, 1966; Feldman & MacCullough, 1971; Masters & Johnson, 1979; McGuire, 1985) with little success. What most reported were changes in behaviors, and they assumed that change in behavior indicated a change in orientation. While behavior may be altered, it is unlikely that orientation can be changed by

any of the psychotherapeutic or other approaches mentioned (Coleman, 1978).

The growing body of literature which refutes the notion that
homosexuality is an illness has assisted in burying the illness model
of treatment. Other authors have noted that homophobia has clearly
existed in the mental health professional community (DeCrescenzo,
1985; Pillard, 1978). Newer models of treatment are less homophobic,
and suggest approaches that are more suitable and appropriate for
adolescent clients.

Cates (1987) notes that, considering the range of dynamics that
may give rise to adolescent homosexuality, a single broad model of
intervention appears inappropriate. Interventions must be tailored to
meet the needs of individual adolescents based on their stage of
development, chronological age, and areas of concern. In addition,
the importance of obtaining a thorough psychosocial history and an
informed understanding of the clients' perceptions of homosexuality cannot be overly emphasized. This is the place to begin before
considering appropriate interventions. The case citations which follow demonstrate the use of varied approaches with adolescent clients.

Most lesbian and gay youth come into an awareness of their
sexual orientation during adolescence (Hunter & Schaecher, 1987;
Malyon, 1981; Remafedi, 1985). Being attracted to someone of the
same gender is a feeling that is emotional, affectional and sexual.
For a gay or lesbian youth, this can be a very frightening time. A
homosexually oriented young person may not be ready or able to
acknowledge his or her sexual orientation, and may initially identify as heterosexual.

Sexual behaviors do not always correspond to sexual identity
(CWLA, 1991). Malyon (1981) notes common adaptations to the
dilemma of sexual identity for the gay adolescent, ranging from
repression to disclosure.

The young lesbian or gay person will face difficulties no matter
which adaptation he or she employs. The repressed youngster may
act out, displaying behaviors which elicit the least satisfactory
results. The suppressed youngster often exhibits identity formation
which is abridged, and is expressed through overachievement, and
compensation for feelings of inadequacy and unacceptability. Dis-

closed, or self-identified gay and lesbian adolescents, are often alienated and neglected by their peers as well as by the larger heterosexual culture. The disclosed group is easiest for most professionals to identify.

Significant numbers of young people identify themselves as bisexual during adolescence, and as homosexual when they become adults. In some instances, this may be due to adolescent sexual experimentation with both genders, while in other instances it stems from a feeling that it is somehow less stigmatizing, and therefore more acceptable, to be seen as bisexual, rather than to be viewed as homosexual.

STIGMATIZATION

The negative effects of stigmatization include social isolation; the development of a sense of difference; the lack of familial support; harassment and violence; and the severe impact of gay-bashing on the mental health of many gay and lesbian adolescents. Clinicians generally agree that the stressors which cause gay and lesbian youth to become emotionally ill originate with society's reaction to sexual orientation, and not from the orientation itself.

Hetrick and Martin (1987), in their frequently cited article, note that in addition to coping with the usual developmental processes of adolescence, the gay and lesbian adolescent's primary developmental task is adjustment to a socially stigmatized role. The authors also note that this sense of isolation occurs on emotional, social and cognitive levels.

Hunter and Schaecher (1990) note:

> It is very difficult to grow up with a positive self image when one's identity carries a stigma. People who are unable to conform to the standards society calls normal are disqualified from full acceptance and are therefore stigmatized. Part of that process has been to label homosexuals as deviant, sick or sinful. (p. 300)

Remafedi (1985) concurs, noting that homosexuality per se is not related to psychopathology or psychological adjustment, rather, it is the social stigma attached to homosexuality that may be injurious (p. 483). The author indicates that changes in performance or behavior in school, at home, or in employment may indicate that the homosexual youngster is at risk for serious psychosocial problems. In his 1987 study of 29 gay male youth, Remafedi reported that 72% of those surveyed had consulted mental health professionals for emotional problems. In a majority of the cases, the problems were related to personal or interpersonal conflict regarding sexual identity. Thirty-one percent of those surveyed had been hospitalized for mental health issues, and in more than half of these cases, hospitalization was precipitated by a suicide attempt. All but one subject admitted that they had contemplated suicide at some time in their lives, while 34% of the subjects had actually attempted suicide, with two having made multiple attempts. Half of those who had attempted suicide directly related it to issues of sexual identity (p. 335).

In their interviews with 60 young homosexual and bisexual men, Roeshler and Deisher (1972) found similar results. Forty-eight percent of those who participated in their study had consulted mental health professionals, and 31% had attempted suicide. See elsewhere in this volume for Durby's discussion of sampling methods, source of statistics on adolescent suicide, and recommendations for research in this area.

HIDING AND ISOLATION

Hiding one's orientation leads to dysfunction and to distortion of relationships, which lead to social isolation and feelings of extreme loneliness. Martin (1982) wrote extensively about the effects of hiding for gay and lesbian adolescents. He wrote:

> The socialization of the gay adolescent becomes a process of deception at all levels. This strategy of deception distorts almost all relationships the adolescent may attempt to develop or maintain and creates a sense of isolation. (p. 58)

One of the major aspects of this sense of isolation is the ever present need to self monitor. Gay and lesbian adolescents who hide are experts at monitoring their conscious and automatic behaviors. The stress of watching the way one talks, stands, carries books, holds their hands, or dresses can become unbearable. Responding to this sense of isolation, and to the psycho-social stressors which it causes, many gay and lesbian adolescents are at risk for depression, feelings of hopelessness and helplessness, low self-esteem and diminished feelings of self-worth, impulsivity, poor coping mechanisms for interpersonal interactions, alcohol and substance abuse to anesthetize their feelings, pregnancies resulting from heterosexual experimentation, dropping out of school, sexually transmitted diseases, homelessness, discrimination in housing, employment and health care services, HIV infection, prostitution, and suicide (Mallon, 1993).

Martin further notes that gay or lesbian adolescents are faced with three choices as they begin to realize that they are part of a stigmatized and despised population. They can hide, they can attempt to change their orientation, or they can accept it. Noting that the third choice would be the most optimal, Martin states that society encourages the homosexually oriented adolescent to adopt the first two strategies. In doing so, gay and lesbian youth are subject to various psychosocial stressors that can cause profound emotional disturbance. As their focus shifts from the home to peer socialization, most adolescents begin to feel a normal distancing between themselves and their families. Gay and lesbian adolescents, however, sometimes experience an abnormal distancing out of fear that their parents will discover their secret. In the absence of appropriate social supports, young homosexual males in particular are at risk for resorting to transient, anonymous, and potentially abusive sexual contacts as their only social outlet. Even anonymous sex is preferred over the alternatives of extreme loneliness and isolation (Martin, 1982).

The following case example illustrates some of the issues regarding the isolation and loneliness experienced by many gay and lesbian adolescents. One painfully shy young man in counseling reported hearing taunts from his family that, "next thing you know he'll be hanging out in Times Square with the other queers." It was not the first time that he had heard Times Square mentioned, and feeling that perhaps this was the place where gay people could meet other gay people, the young man headed for Forty-Second Street, in hopes of finding others like him. What he encountered, instead, were older men who were willing to pay him money for sex, and anonymous sex which could be found in "bookstores" and "peep shows." Even though these activities at first made him uncomfortable and also included a dangerous element of hiding and secretiveness, he found them to be a preferable alternative to the loneliness and isolation that he had thus far experienced. He was referred for counseling by a school guidance counselor, who did not feel competent to address the issue of his sexual orientation. The counseling focused on his isolation and feelings of loneliness. In an effort to decrease feelings of loneliness and promote appropriate social behavior, the counselor referred him to a local gay and lesbian social services agency, where the young man could engage in healthier, non-sexual, social activities, and where he could meet other gay and lesbian young people. Though socialization options are limited, and role models of productive relationships are difficult to find, this young man was nonetheless encouraged to seek out both. His use of sexual activity within friendships and as casual encounters was also addressed in treatment. He recognized his ambivalence, using sex as a means to deal with his loneliness. Given the risk of contracting the HIV virus, generally thought to be the cause of AIDS, mental health professionals have an obligation to address this risk factor in the course of psychotherapy. In the form of direct education, this young man was cautioned about the need to reduce higher risk sex as well as the potential consequences of unsafe sex for himself and his partners.

A SENSE OF DIFFERENTNESS

Most young gay and lesbian people sense a "differentness" about themselves that stems from conflict between the gender identity role expected by society and by most families, and the individual's inner sense of gender identity role (Hunter & Schaecher, 1990). The sexual attraction for same-sex partners which is felt by the lesbian and gay adolescent violates a fundamental norm of society. Society expects that one is attracted to the opposite sex, eventually falls in love, gets married and has children. When adolescents who are lesbian and gay begin to realize that this is not what they will experience, it can cause conflict and concern. One 19-year-old lesbian related the following:

> I always knew that I was a dyke. My mother was always trying to get me to dress more like a girl, you know, dresses and all. Once in a while I would just do it to make her happy, but I always felt so uncomfortable. Before I came out, I was in denial, I used to also say that I liked boys, I even went out with a few of them on dates, but, they never did anything for me. I'd try to get into kissing them and all that, but, I knew that inside it was girls that really did something for me. When I finally came out, my friend really helped me, I realized that this is who I am, I am a dyke and that's just who I am and now I know why I felt different.

Of course, many gay and lesbian adolescents and adults as well are gender typical in their mannerisms, attire, and general presentation of self in the world. It would be incorrect to assume that all lesbians and gays, by definition, behave in gender non-typical ways.

LACK OF FAMILIAL SUPPORT

For many years, parents have been misinformed that it was their role modeling and behavior, including parenting style, that determined whether or not their child would grow up to be gay or lesbian. It is no wonder that parental reaction to a child's disclosure can include anger, denial, guilt, insistence on therapy to "change" the young person's orientation, and in some cases, abuse. Disclosure can also cause expulsion from the home. Fearing rejection, the young person will usually hide his or her sexual orientation as long as is possible. Sometimes this pressure becomes too great, and the young person may attempt suicide (Hunter & Schaecher, 1990, p. 302). Often, a conspiracy of silence develops within the family, and the unspoken rule becomes, "no one is permitted to talk about it." One 18-year-old man described it this way: "They know, but we don't talk about it. I tried to sit down and talk with them, answer their questions, but they wouldn't hear of it. All my father said was, it made him want to puke . . . my mother just cried."

The continued lack of family support creates many problems for the gay or lesbian adolescent, and negatively impacts their emotional and cognitive development. The same young man continued saying:

> When I realized that my own family couldn't accept me, my own flesh and blood, I thought, why should I expect the rest of society to cut me any slack? I felt hopeless, disillusioned and worthless. My own family . . . how could they do that to me, be so cold, so uncaring. It was as if they were saying they didn't care if I lived or died. I don't think I'll ever get over that.

This young man was clearly in need of support, but was also clearly at risk for suicidal ideation. Nonacceptance of the adolescent's homosexuality leads to alienation from the family, which can often result in attempted or completed suicide (Hunter & Schaecher, 1987). Counseling focused on building this young person's self-esteem and monitored his feelings of hopelessness, worthlessness and depression. A variety of empathic psychotherapeutic approaches were utilized in twice weekly sessions. Contracting was also utilized to insure that he would not harm himself.

HARASSMENT AND VIOLENCE

Gay and lesbian youth are at high risk for harassment and violence by family, neighbors, and peers. In a study investigating violence against lesbians and gay male youth, Hunter (1990) reported that 41% of a sample of 500 gay males reported having suffered violence by families, peers, or strangers. Nearly half of the violence was gay-related. While many young people report that verbal harassment is so frequent that it is a given, they also note that it can sometimes escalate into physical violence (Mallon, 1992). One 16-year-old lesbian put it this way:

> Every day when I came home from school, I had to pass by this rough area in my neighborhood where all of these guys always hung out. They were always yelling out things to me, like: 'Yo, bull dagger, hey, where's your motorcycle. They'd

make motorcycle noises and laugh at me.' You know, stupid stuff like that. But I got so sick of it, I mean I just couldn't take it anymore, I was just walking home minding my own business. One day though, I couldn't take it anymore and I went up to them and asked them to please just lay off and leave me alone. I was real scared doing that, I mean they could have jumped me or messed me up or something, but I had to say something, I wasn't going to let them do this to me anymore. I don't think they expected it when I walked right up to them, and after that I got some respect. I'm glad that they don't harass me so much anymore, I mean I'm glad I got that respect, but I shouldn't have to earn it like that. I mean, I shouldn't have to confront people for just being who I am. I should get respect because I am a person, just like they are.

This young woman had a strong sense of her identity and a great deal of courage as well. While her approach to resolving this verbal harassment worked for her on this occasion, she also put herself at great risk by walking up to this group of young men by herself. One option she might have considered was filing a complaint at the local Anti-Violence Project. Her treatment also focused on other possible strategies for dealing with future harassment situations. Having an inner sense of self-esteem can assist young people in approaching verbal harassment from a rational perspective, but they also must remember that not all of those who initiate the harassment are people who are rational, or who can always be counted on to behave rationally.

MODERN COUNSELING INTERVENTION STRATEGIES

Coleman (1978) notes that, prior to the civil rights and gay rights movement, most homosexuals who consulted mental health professionals were encouraged to change their orientation. Very few came to therapists asking that their orientation be left intact (p. 86-87). Historian and gay rights activist, Martin Duberman, has written a very personal and moving account of this process in his book entitled, *Cures: A Gay Man's Odyssey.*

As times have changed, those who have been sensitized within the mental health professions have accepted that most effective interventions for gay and lesbian adolescents are based on enhancing how one feels about oneself, rather than on trying to eliminate homosexuality. Individual and group approaches which emphasize trust, openness, expression of feelings, and exploration of feelings of intimacy are most successful. The main objective of all counseling interventions is to help the client function more fully as a human being. For gay and lesbian adolescents, caught in a whirl of constant change and transformation, this objective may need to be modified to meet individual needs.

SUGGESTIONS FOR EFFECTIVELY COUNSELING GAY AND LESBIAN ADOLESCENTS

The most important factor for mental health professionals when working with gay and lesbian adolescent clients is that the therapist must be supportive of the adolescent, and must feel comfortable with the issues of homosexuality and sexuality in general, including the therapist's own sexuality. The following suggestions may be helpful:

1. While gay and lesbian professionals will undoubtedly have special insights into the experience of the gay and lesbian adolescent, being gay or lesbian is not necessarily a prerequisite for counseling this population. Both homosexual and heterosexual counselors can be effective in addressing the clinical needs of this population. Having an accurate knowledge of the population, as well as being understanding, empathic, and giving non-biased, non-judgmental advice are attributes which are essential when counseling a gay or lesbian youth.

2. A basic social work principle states that workers should meet clients where they are. Let the client know that it is okay to be bisexual, gay or lesbian, that it is okay to be confused, and to not enter into a relationship. It is also okay for the client to go back and forth and change his or her mind.

3. Help the clients to understand and clarify their feelings about their orientation.

4. The counselor should be able to provide accurate and adequate information, which is readable and understandable, to the

young person. Literature written by gay and lesbian young people for gay and lesbian young people is most helpful (Alyson, 1991; Frick, 1983; Heron, 1983; Miranda, 1993). This information should assist the homosexually oriented youngster in abolishing myths and stereotypes.

5. Provide, or be able to refer youngsters to non-sexually charged, healthy peer support groups within their local communities or schools, when these are available. Social interaction among other gay and lesbian youth will help to alleviate the social isolation and loneliness which most gay and lesbian adolescents experience.

6. Help clients to develop other appropriate contacts within the gay and lesbian community. Counselors should educate themselves about these resources and be able to refer clients to them.

7. Help the client to develop effective interpersonal coping mechanisms to deal with the negative effects of societal stigmatization. Assist young people in exploring and developing mechanisms to deal with conflict, relationships, depression, safer sex, and peer pressures.

8. Be aware of the signs of suicidal ideation, alcohol and other substance abuse. Know the resources to which clients can be referred for dealing with these issues.

9. Help the client to deal with a wide variety of family issues, and be prepared to help families also. Whenever possible, young people should be helped to reunite or reconcile with their families; if this is not possible, then help the young person to find a supportive gay-affirming placement, and assist them in developing life skills to enable them to live independently. Counselors should proceed cautiously in assisting gay and lesbian youngsters who want to disclose their orientation to their families. There should be a thorough discussion of the risks involved, as well as the advantages, since no one can know in advance how a family will respond.

10. Train other professionals by providing them with accurate and adequate information about homosexual adolescent issues. Help other professionals to view homosexuality from a non-judgmental, non-pejorative perspective.

11. Be prepared to be an advocate for the youngster who is having trouble at school, in a group or foster home, or in their own fam-

ily. The protection of the gay and lesbian youth is an important task for the counselor.

12. While it is important for the gay and lesbian young person to have role models, adults who counsel them must be careful to set and maintain professional boundaries which protect both the adult and the young person. Social interaction outside of the counseling session should be avoided.

13. Respect confidentiality at all times. The relationship must be based on trust, understanding, and respect.

CONCLUSIONS

The clinical issues which confront gay and lesbian adolescents seeking mental health care services are rooted, in part, in their adjustment to a stigmatized role in a society which teaches them that they belong to a group which is despised and hated. For many years, since most homosexually oriented people sought professional help to change their orientation, the illness model of homosexuality was utilized in treating the emotional distress of the gay and lesbian person. Aversion therapy, conversion, and desensitization therapies have also been used, with little success. Many gay and lesbian people have suggested that it is homophobia which really needs to be cured, not homosexuality.

Gay and lesbian youth struggle with the same problems as other adolescents, but also with those which are unique to anyone who is homosexually-oriented. The stress of societal stigmatization and of hiding one's orientation leads to social, emotional and cognitive isolation and intense feelings of loneliness, depression, hopelessness, low self-esteem, and worthlessness. A sense of differentness can add to these feelings. In addition, the stress of dealing with family rejection, verbal harassment, and physical violence, can lead to emotional distress and even to suicide attempts or completions. The most effective interventions with the gay and lesbian adolescent assist these young people in developing strategies to enhance their homosexuality, not to eliminate it. Those who work with gay and lesbian adolescents must be comfortable addressing issues of homosexuality and be open to developing individualized treatment plans, using a variety of approaches designed to address the unique needs of each client.

Helping young people grow into healthy, well adjusted adults is one of the primary goals of youth work. Most young people have caring families to guide them on this journey. Some gay and lesbian young people are more distant from their families than heterosexually oriented teenagers and, in some instances, are completely rejected by their families and, as a result, need other caring adults in their lives to help them to complete the journey into adulthood successfully. The challenges of adolescence are daunting for all youth, but can be especially disheartening for gay and lesbian youth, who face special and difficult tests on their way to adulthood. Many of the clinical manifestations of emotional distress presented by these youth in treatment are the result of attempts to cope with being different in a homophobic society. Consequently, it is important for youth workers, social workers, and other mental health professionals to be aware of, and sensitive to, the unique environmental stressors which impact gay and lesbian youth. Additionally, clinicians particularly, and all youth workers generally, should avail themselves of special training focused on clinical issues common to many gay and lesbian youth.

REFERENCES

Alyson, S. (Ed.). (1991). *Young, gay and proud.* Boston: Alyson Publications.

Bieber, I., Dain, H.J., Dince, P.R., Drellich, M.G., Grand, H.G., Gundlach, R.H., Kremer, M.W., Rifkin, A.H., Wilbur, C.B., & Bieber, T.B. (1962). *Homosexuality: A Psychoanalytic study.* New York: Basic Books.

Cates, J.A. (1987). Adolescent sexuality: Gay and lesbian issues. *Child Welfare League of America, 66,* 353-363.

Cautela, J. (1967). Covert sensitization. *Psychological Reports, 20,* 459-468.

Child Welfare League of America. (1991). *Serving the needs of gay and lesbian youth: The role of child welfare agencies, recommendations of a colloquium-January 25-26, 1991.* Washington, DC: Child Welfare League of America.

Coleman, E. (1978). Toward a new model of treatment of homosexuality: A review. *Journal of Homosexuality, 3,* 345-359.

DeCrescenzo, T. (1979). Group work with gay adolescents. *Journal of Social Work with Groups 2* (1), New York: The Haworth Press, Inc.

DeCrescenzo, T. (1985). Homophobia: A study of the attitudes of mental health professionals toward homosexuality. In R. Schoenberg, R. Goldberg, & D.

Shore (Eds.), *With compassion toward some: Homosexuality and social work in America*, (pp. 115-136). New York: Harrington Park Press.

Duberman, M. (1991). *Cures: A gay man's odyssey*. New York: Dutton.

Feldman, M. (1966). Aversion therapy for sexual deviation: A critical review. *Psychological Bulletin, 65*, 65-69.

Feldman, M. & MacCullough, M.J. (1965). The application of anticipatory avoidance learning to the treatment of homosexuality: Theory, technique, and preliminary results. *Behavior Research and Therapy, 2*, 165-183.

Frick, A. (1983). *Reflections of a rock lobster: A story about growing up gay*. Boston, MA: Alyson Publications.

Heron, A. (Ed.). (1983). *One teenager in 10*. Boston: Alyson Press.

Hetrick, E. & Martin, A.D. (1987). Developmental issues and their resolution for gay and lesbian adolescents. *The Journal of Homosexuality, 13*(4), 25-43.

Hunter, J. (1990). Violence against lesbian and gay male youths. *Journal of Interpersonal Violence, 5*(3), 295-300.

Hunter, J. & Schaecher, R. (1987). Stresses on lesbian and gay adolescents in schools. *Social Work in Education*, Spring, Vol. 9, 180-188.

Hunter, J. & Schaecher, R. (1990). Lesbian and gay youth. In M.J. Rotherram-Borus, J. Bradley, & N. Obolensky (Eds.). *Planning to live–Evaluating and treating suicidal teens in community settings*, (pp. 297-316). Tulsa: University of Oklahoma Press.

Mallon, G.P. (1992). Gay and no place to go: Assessing the needs of gay and lesbian adolescents in out-of-home care settings. *Child Welfare, 71*(6), 547-556.

Mallon, G.P. (1993). An open discussion about gay and lesbian adolescents in out-of-home child welfare settings. *Daily Living, 7*(2), 4-5.

Malyon, A.K. (1981). The homosexual adolescent: Developmental issues and social bias. *Child Welfare League of America, 60*(5), 321-330.

Martin, A.D. (1982). Learning to hide: The socialization of the gay adolescent. In S.C. Feinstein, J.G. Looney, A. Schartzberg, & A. Sorosky (Eds.), *Adolescent psychiatry: Developmental and clinical studies, 10*. Chicago: University of Chicago Press.

Masters, W.H. & Johnson, V.E. (1979). *Homosexuality in perspective*. Boston: Little, Brown.

Mayerson, P. & Lief, H. (1965). Psychotherapy of homosexuals: A follow-up study of nineteen cases. In J. Marmor (Ed.), *Sexual inversion*. New York: Basic Books.

McGuire, W.J. (1985). Attitudes and attitude change. In G. Lindzey & E. Aronson (Eds.), *Handbook of social psychology, 2*, (pp. 233-246). New York: Random House.

Mercier, L.R. & Berger, R.M. (1989). Social service needs of lesbian and gay adolescents: Telling it their way. In G. Remafedi (Ed.), *Adolescent challenges: New challenges for social work*, (pp. 75-97). New York: The Haworth Press, Inc.

Miranda, D. (1993, May & June). I hated myself. *New Youth Connections*, p. 8.

Needham, R. (1977). Casework intervention with a homosexual adolescent. *Social Casework, 58,* 387-394.

Pillard, R. (1978). Psychotherapeutic treatment for the invisible minority. *Psychiatric Annals, 18*(1), 99-113.

Remafedi, G. (1985). Adolescent homosexuality: Issues for pediatricians. *Clinical Pediatrics, 24*(9), 481-485.

Remafedi, G. (1987a). Male homosexuality: The adolescent's perspective. *Pediatrics, 79,* 326-330.

Remafedi, G. (1987b). Homosexual youth: A challenge to contemporary society. *Journal of the American Medical Association, 258*(2), 222-228.

Roeshler, T. & Deisher, R.W. (1972). Youthful male homosexuality: Homosexual experience and the process of developing homosexual identity in males ages 16 to 22 years, *Journal of the American Medical Association, 219,* 1018-1023.

Schneider, M. (1988). *Often invisible: Counseling gay and lesbian youth.* Toronto: Toronto Central Youth Services.

Whitlock, K. (1989). *Bridges of respect.* Philadelphia: American Friends Service Committee.

Developmental Implications
of Homophobia
for Lesbian and Gay Adolescents:
Issues in Policy and Practice

Darryl Jackson
Richard Sullivan

SUMMARY. This essay seeks to provide a critical analysis of how the developmental obstacles faced by lesbian and gay adolescents and the limitations on helping them are both byproducts of institutionalized homophobia. Implications for ethical practice grounded in advocacy are presented. Adolescence is above all else a transition to a more complex set of roles which have to be integrated into the totality of the self. We argue that most of the difficulties identified among sexual minority youth need not burden their development, and that it is an obligation of the helping professions to work toward the eradication of encumbrances to their optimal development. That work must begin with a critical analysis of our own theories and perspectives.

Theories of human development and the professions that draw on those theories are no more insulated from the biases of the cultures

Darryl Jackson, MSW, is a Vancouver social worker whose current professional activities include the development of a needs assessment for social development in the gay and lesbian community in Vancouver, Canada.

Richard Sullivan, DSW, is Assistant Professor of Social Work at the University of British Columbia, in Vancouver, Canada.

[Haworth co-indexing entry note]: "Developmental Implications of Homophobia for Lesbian and Gay Adolescents: Issues in Policy and Practice." Jackson, Darryl, and Richard Sullivan. Co-published simultaneously in *Journal of Gay & Lesbian Social Services* (The Haworth Press, Inc.) Vol. 1, No. 3/4, 1994, pp. 93-109; and: *Helping Gay and Lesbian Youth: New Policies, New Programs, New Practice* (ed: Teresa DeCrescenzo) The Haworth Press, Inc., 1994, pp. 93-109. Multiple copies of this article/chapter may be purchased from The Haworth Document Delivery Center [1-800-3-HAWORTH; 9:00 a.m. - 5:00 p.m. (EST)].

in which they develop than any other social institution. Developmental norms and diagnostic categories change not just as a function of new knowledge, but also as a function of shifting social values, ideologies and sociopolitical contingencies. This has been nowhere more evident than with homosexuality, which has been variously treated as a legal or moral offense, a psychiatric disorder, and a normal variant within the range of human sexual responses. Every period has its prevailing wisdom and research findings that contradict that wisdom do not readily change public perceptions. The sociopolitical context in which new knowledge emerges must be receptive to the possibility of a changed perception and an alteration of the social roles and values associated with the particular group in question. Empirical evidence provides no support for either psychiatric classification or social opprobrium in the case of homosexuals. Nonetheless, as in other historical periods, elective ignorance and the vilification of a particular minority group has served to sustain the privileges of some at the expense of others. The absence or denial of accurate information operates as an influence in the developmental course of gay and lesbian adolescents. It also affects the competence of those to whom these youths might turn for assistance.

Competent practice requires the practitioner to assess the impact of the adolecent's transactions with the environment on the elaboration of developmental processes. When the environment is hostile to some aspect of the adolescent's developing identity, the impact of that hostility on the reflected self-appraisals of the individual must be understood as a potential obstacle to the integration of a positive self-identity. As Troiden (1988) suggests, self-concept is a composite of situationally determined identities related to the performance of a variety of social roles. The perceived value of those roles and the reflected self-appraisal of one's skill in performing those roles affect the attractiveness of the role and hence the desirability of mastering knowledge and skills related to that role. Social marginalization and the denial of accurate, corrective information to counter negative stereotypes may encumber social development and the cognitive apprehension of possibilities for the youth whose identity is potentially compromised by stigma. In this essay, we identify social and cognitive development as two areas in which stigma and devaluation may challenge the development of lesbian and gay adolescents' mastery of skills related to the negotiation of their minority status and we review some of the adaptations they may make to that challenge.

DEVELOPMENTAL TASKS AND OBSTACLES FOR LESBIAN AND GAY ADOLESCENTS

To begin with, adolescence should be understood as a transitional stage like other transitional stages. The transitional process ought to allow the adolescent to gradually adjust to growth and development. It should be a period in which crisis is avoided by allowing for the gradual adjustment to biological, cognitive, psychological and social changes within a context of familial stability. As with all other life transitions, adolescence brings challenges and opportunities which are mediated by the existing personality structure and contribute to the ongoing elaboration of that structure.

The course of adolescence is benign for most children, despite the histrionics of some developmental theories and the exaggerated perceptions of those who work with clinical populations (Boxer and Cohler, 1989). The presumed inevitability of an identity crisis is a social construct and like most social constructions, it is neither inevitable nor necessary. For lesbian and gay youth, however, problems related to the integration of all aspects of their identity, including a positive sexual identity, may be more probable. That probability has been found to increase as the experience of homophobia, social isolation and degradation increases and the prospect of positive role identifications decreases (Remafedi, 1987; Ross, 1989). There has been little systematic longitudinal study of the adjustment of lesbian and gay adolescents, however, and that void is itself reflective of the marginality of these youths. The invisibility to which they have been consigned is an artifact of historical, cultural, socioeconomic, and political factors related to each other on the common ground of homophobia. Potential devaluation is never less than a latent obstacle to some aspects of their cognitive and social development. The dynamic this introduces to the social transactions and self-appraisals of sexual minority youth must be understood by anyone seeking to guide them through the shoals of adolescence.

COGNITIVE DEVELOPMENT

Among the changes which occur during this transition is a change in the direction of cognitive processes. In Piagetian terms, this is the shift from concrete operational thought to formal operations. Formal thought involves reasoning that is based on the capacity to make hypothetical deductions and to entertain the idea of relativity. Grasping the relative, that is, truly entertaining the relative merits of a range of possibilities, rests on a reversal in the young person's consideration of reality and possibility. Whereas children's sense of the possible derives solely from their own experience and observation of reality, the transition to formal operational thinking implies an ability to begin with a theoretical synthesis of what is possible and then proceed to a consideration of what is empirically real (Offer and Sabshin, 1984).

The cognitive readiness to differentiate among the possibilities one encounters in the world rests on a continuity of selfhood. In other words, the readiness to consider differences in the world can be present only when the child has confidence in the stability, integrity and continuity of his/her own identity. When one knows who one is, one can consider the selves of others who are not like us but whose unique selves can be considered valid and not threatening to our own identity. The very achievement of object permanence in early childhood and identity permanence in later childhood (adolescence) transpires through ongoing experimentation, through imitation and the selective internalization of others' values and beliefs, and through the cumulative realization that one's self is both similar to and separate from others (ibid. p. 87).

The perceived acceptability of those aspects of the self that are separate or different from others affects the aversion or affinity with which the person approaches the identification and integration of the feelings, beliefs and other concomitants of a perceived role. Where aversion dominates, those feelings and beliefs are less often subjected to the highest level of rational scrutiny. Rather, rational examination is averted, convention is sustained, and latent or imminent possibilities go immediately unexplored. This is true for intellectual, athletic and artistic proclivities as well. If not valued, they may remain latent possibilities. In other words, the exploration of

these possible identities is thwarted by devaluation. Therefore, investment in the social and cognitive mastery of these roles is diminished. Knowledge and relevant social skills are averted along with
devaluation. These will not be the roles and identities with which
the adolescent undertakes her/his apprenticeship in adult society.
They will not be a priority for skill development or even for understanding.

This does not imply that lesbian and gay youth arrive at early
adulthood necessarily disadvantaged or delayed. Avoidance of intimacy and potential conflicts and dysphoria related to sexuality may
incline the youth to other pursuits, but a realistic grasp and integration of their full potential as interactive beings may be diverted.
Social competence may be compromised by the unavailability of
opportunities for meaningful practice in contexts relevant to their
own integration of desire and possibility. Unlike other proclivities,
powerful instinctual feelings fuel the exploration of the possible
with respect to sexuality and conflict can therefore be postponed but
never entirely eliminated.

SOCIAL DEVELOPMENT

A child's capacity to try on the roles of others, to empathize with
others and consider their reality develops through a process of
exposure to differences of opinion, the need to communicate with
others, and the experience of encountering valued others whose
views are resolutely different from our own. At this stage, we move
away from the egocentrism of childhood and observe a new capacity for decentering which involves striving for self consistency
while also trying on new ideas about ourselves. The possibility
emerges in adolescence to reject others' views and definitions of
oneself. There is a concomitant loneliness inherent in the process of
giving up others' definitions of us and beginning to forge new
definitions. That transitory aloneness as a self-conscious separation/
individuation process, is a normal component of the usually mild
depression and insecurity that many adolescents experience at some
point in their transition to young adulthood. It is mediated by peer
support and an expanding horizon of potential identities.

For many adolescents the possibilities are endless and that in itself may be overwhelming. For others, there are no apparent possibilities or existing possibilities are devalued. There is no role available to fit the subjective experience of who one is. There is no apparent path for the integration of desire and possibility. That is why the repression of visible gay role models in every profession is dangerous, not only for those professions but for the children for whom those gay teachers, doctors and social workers may provide hope and possibility. That explicit repression tells a significant number of adolescents that they can have no future, no vision, no role models, no possibilities. This obliteration of possible positive identifications and role models is dangerous for all minority youth.

Adolescence is above all else a transition to a more complex set of roles which have to be integrated into the totality of the self. It is a period in which we practice and hone the relationship skills that prepare us for adult partnerships, along with the work habits and problem solving skills that will enable us to set goals and achieve them. All of this rests on a belief in one's own future and on the integrity of self-definition. If we accept that the integration of identity is a crucial element in this transition, then how can we suggest that the transition is benign for the majority of gay and lesbian adolescents? Faced with clear social messages of their unacceptability, how can they arrive at adulthood relatively unscathed? The fact that so many do so bespeaks an adaptive strength and coping mechanisms that must be understood, validated and enhanced in these young people. The assessment of the coping skills that foster resiliency is important to understanding the course of child development (Boxer and Cohler, 1989).

OBSTACLES AND MEDIATING STRUCTURES

Like all normal, healthy young persons, the gay or lesbian adolescent can gain some distance from the need for other people's esteem by increasing social competence and the capacity for self-validation. For the child who must keep a secret, the successful management of a potentially spoiled identity reflects a level of social skill and pain management that is deserving of self-validation. That self-validation can be facilitated and enhanced by supportive professionals and by significant others with whom the adolescent can feel safe in sharing the secret. The buffering effects of family and community in protecting the self-esteem and sustaining the motivation of other minority children can provide some valuable lessons for the helping professional who is working to sustain the motivation for continuing forward striving in the gay or lesbian adolescent. As Powell and her colleagues (1983) have noted, this is much easier when the family buffers the child's developing ego against the assaults of a prejudicial society as part of its role in socializing the child to safe functioning in a sometimes hostile world. The parents of lesbian and gay youth may be less able to do that because their own experience is less likely to have prepared them for that role. They may well bear the prejudices of the majority, and their child's sexual orientation may remain unknown to them if the child perceives their support and approval to be unavailable. Assessing parental homophobia then becomes an important part of working with families confronted with the need to reformulate some aspects of their conception of their child. Where homophobia is present, it may be necessary to help parents identify the ways in which their child is no different than before the disclosure and to identify the areas in which their approval is still immediately available. In other words, parents may need to compartmentalize as part of the process of adjustment. Until the youth has achieved the independence and ego strength to make more situationally-determined choices about disclosure, the professional helper can play a key role in assisting the adolescent to gain a measure of distance from social devaluation through the enhancement of self-approval.

No one can entirely eliminate the need for other people's approval. The capacity to approve of oneself derives from stable, unqualified acceptance by someone. For the adolescent who is stigmatized among peers, this may mean that he or she cannot risk parental disapproval. These will be the children who are extremely compliant at home or at school, in many ways the ideal children, never risking parental judgement or rejection by testing their own will and their own identity (Gonsiorek, 1988). Unconscious parental collusion supports the protracted dependence of these youths within a family system that serves as a refuge from the world of their contemporaries, a world in which they do not enjoy a subjective sense of belonging. There is a gay and lesbian community in which peers can be found to validate and reintegrate identity, but for the most part that is an adult social system that remains unavailable to the adolescent. In the interim, the capacity for self-validation can be enhanced by a supportive, accepting adult but responsible practice at both the individual level and at the policy level cannot ignore the need to create opportunities for peer socialization among an otherwise isolated minority.

For isolated youngsters who are without peers and have not had an opportunity to internalize any role models or ego ideals, it is all the more important that they have aspects of themselves that they value and that are validated by significant others. Disclosure that results in parental rejection makes these children all the more vulnerable to fragmented or delayed integration of identity, diminished self-esteem, and sometimes outright abuse, rejection, and exploitation (Borhek, 1988; Savin-Williams, 1989; Strommen, 1990). A teenager who can hide, who has the support of his peers or, better yet, who doesn't have to hide and still has the support of his/her peers can better withstand the test of wills that so often accompanies an adolescent's assertion of a separate identity. The adolescent who has no other support can least afford to lose her/his parents at this time.

For the child who has no close peer relationships, the internalization of a positive ego-ideal can also be facilitated through literature. Role models do not necessarily have to be people we are in direct contact with. Fortunately, there is a growing body of literature which can provide positive role models for gay and lesbian adolescents. Unfortunately, that literature is not generally available to them in their schools or public libraries. The current censorship campaign mobilized by conservative religious ideologues stands to illustrate the campaign of oblivion that confronts these youths' search for self-definition and meaning.

ADAPTATION AND THE 'COMING-OUT' PROCESS

The integration of various aspects of identity in the transition to young adulthood presents special problems for the gay or lesbian adolescent. Since sexual desires cannot be entirely repressed from awareness without psychic cost, the sexual minority teenager often learns to compartmentalize sexual desire, leading to developmental adaptations wherein there is a moratorium on some developmental tasks–including identity integration (Troiden, 1988). Several authors have explored the unique developmental challenges faced by lesbian and gay youth in relation to the coming-out process (Cass, 1979; Minton and McDonald, 1984; Gonsiorek, 1988; Reiter, 1989). The stages of adaptation to a homosexual identity are commonly conceived to include the following four options, often negotiated sequentially, though developmental adaptation may terminate at any stage:

1. The repression of same sex desire. This requires great intra-psychic energy and is rarely sustained without cost. Effects may include emotional constriction of one's ability to relate intimately to another, loss of identity, disregard for personal needs, or destructive patterns of caretaking others. Less powerful defenses may also be mobilized; over-compensation for feelings of inferiority may produce the compliant over-achiever, the macho risk-taker, or the compulsively perfect daughter. These children lose opportunities to develop inter-personal social skills.
2. A developmental moratorium in which homosexual impulses are suppressed in favor of a heterosexual or asexual orientation (Herdt, 1989). Since conventional assumptions about homosexuality have been internalized uncritically at this stage, homophobia exerts a toxic influence both internally and externally. Failure of suppression may produce profound guilt and depression, sometimes reflected in self-destructive behaviors.
3. The adoption of homosexual behavior without homosexual identity. Here, too, differences in the degree and expression of homophobia along with other sociocultural variables produce cultural variations in the plausibility and sustainability of this option. Some argue that the fusion of behavior and role identity in the social construction of homosexuality did not emerge in Western European cultures until the late 19th century, largely in response to the medicalization and stigmatization of sexual nonconformity (Foucault, 1980).
4. Homosexual disclosure and the integration of same sex desires as part of one's identity. At this point the individual begins to

actively negotiate a homophobic environment through selective disclosure and the self-conscious construction of a social life.

For some adolescents, learning to compartmentalize their various social roles is a positive adaptive strategy and one in which they can be supported in developing the skills to achieve. This can be done within the context of a helping relationship that affirms the integrity of their whole being, while achieving a temporary, conscious compartmentalization. This implies methods of intervention which are consistent with the biphasic course of development for many sexual minority youth. Group work, for example, may provide opportunities for practicing new identities in a safe environment.

Under the best circumstances, people negotiate developmental transitions at the point when their adaptive skills are congruent with the demands of that transition. Delayed negotiation of developmental tasks may produce a developmental moratorium or deficits related to lost opportunities. Similarly, premature confrontation with developmental challenges, particularly in a non-supportive environment, may place the young person at risk (Herdt, 1989). The adoption of either of the first two of the above options may result in an adaptive style characterized by assiduous self-censoring and exaggerated identification with stereotyped gender roles. Premature self-disclosure, particularly in a hostile environment, may result in identity foreclosure. Then in the absence of accurate information and corrective experiences, the adolescent may grasp the only homosexual roles afforded her/him. Their self presentation is then often marked initially by an exaggerated identification with erroneous stereotypes.

The adolescent, bereft of identity up to this point, attaches to the only identity available. In the worst circumstances, that identity is constructed of the myths that signal his/her disaffiliation. Self-presentation may then be marked by a flamboyance that provokes reaction. Anxiety associated with that latent reaction may be relieved by confronting it. In the adherence to the worst possible stereotype, there is sometimes a component of oppositional ("in your face") effrontery. The latter may present some transferential challenges for the professional helper. On one hand we may be embarrassed by the youth's presentation of the stigmatized self, and on the other we may identify with their implicit rebellion. Rebellion and the self-affirming anger that sustains it are both valid and useful when the client has the strength and skill to endure the reaction that his/her insurgency will provoke. The child who is acting out a stereotype because he or she has no other identity and hasn't the skill to hide successfully may not always have the strength to withstand the fire he/she will draw.

Creating an environment that affirms the integration of identity within the broader social context is the responsibility of the helping professional. Going beyond paternalism requires efforts to expand the recognition and influence of lesbian and gay people in shaping the social agenda in their own interests. There is an ethical imperative to adopt an affirmative approach to practice with this vulnerable population. Ultimately, exposure to corrective experiences and a critical analysis of prevailing prejudices foster the resiliency and adaptability by which the majority of gay youth arrive at adulthood. That adaptability stands as evidence that the appropriate focus of intervention is the developmental obstacles that might impede optimal adaptation. By implication the eradication of homophobia in its multiple forms stands as an ethical obligation for the youth-serving professional.

Homophobia has assumed the proportions of a social pathology in our culture. It is codified in law, social policy, religious beliefs and child-rearing practices. The internalization of homophobia can only do damage to self-esteem and the self-concept when it encounters an awareness of homosexual desire. In considering the dysphoria that may result, the traditional approach in treatment is to address the homosexuality and not the homophobia. The homophobia, however, derives from social-transactional phenomena and is therefore at least theoretically more accessible and quite appropriately the focus of intervention. The helping professions are habituated to a view of homosexuality that sees it as the outcome of earlier conflicts instead of seeing the homophobic dysphoria as the product of transactional conflict in the present. The latter requires a more active assumption of responsibility for redressing the disadvantages that place the client at risk. To be effective in assisting the homosexual client to affirm her/his identity in the face of social devaluation, requires that the professional helper have an analysis of that process that affords the client a corrective alternative. Competent practice with minority youth requires no less. Ethical practice must go a step further and act to affect equitable policy.

THE HISTORICAL BASIS AND CONTEMPORARY CONSEQUENCES OF HOMOPHOBIA

In order to understand how homophobia infuses the policies and practices that affect gay and lesbian people, it is necessary to review the modern history of the development of the gay minority. While some authors argue that homosexuality has existed since ancient times (Duberman, Vicinus, and Chauncey, 1989), others have argued that the idea of homosexuality as a stable self-identity did not emerge in the western world until the late seventeenth century (Troiden, 1988). In fact, the word homosexual was coined in 1869 by Karoly Benkert, a Hungarian, with the first references to the word in the English language appearing in the late nineteenth century in the work of sexologist Havelock Ellis (Troiden, 1988). Prior to the emergence of homosexuality as a personal identity, it had been assumed that there was only one sexual identity, that of heterosexual. Heterosexuals could, if they chose to, commit homosexual acts, but they were not in and of themselves thought to be homosexual.

Our understanding of homosexuality, at least in most of the western world, has been extensively influenced by Christianity. The Bible clearly stipulates that homosexual acts are a moral crime—one that is punishable by death:

> If a man also lie with mankind, as lieth with a woman, both of them have committed an abomination: They shall surely be put to death; their blood shall be upon them. (Leviticus, 20:13)

It is little wonder then historically, that men and women who felt disposed towards homoerotic behaviors, chose not to live their lives in such a way as to explicitly state their primary sexual orientation.

The church's impact on homosexuals is difficult to understate. Its position constructed the belief that homosexuals were deviant, and worthy of angry punishment. Existing laws pertaining to homosexuality were strengthened in the nineteenth century, based on religious moral principles, that sought to eliminate homosexual conduct. Such laws referred to homosexuality as unnatural conduct, perversion, a threat to families and children, and a crime against nature (Rivera, 1991).

Condemnatory religious dogma had a secular complement in the emergent psychoanalytic theories of Victorian Europe. There is evidence that Freud himself was not trying to persecute homosexuals, though his paternalistic views were ultimately no less marginalizing:

> Homosexuality is assuredly no advantage, but it is nothing to be ashamed of, no vice, no degradation; we consider it to be a variation of the sexual function, produced by a certain arrest of development . . . It is a great injustice to persecute homosexuality as a crime–and cruelty too . . . (quoted in Savin-Williams, 1988, p. 88)

Freud's theory described the development of homosexuality as a developmental deviance from heterosexuality. It was the natural continuation of what the church had been teaching for centuries, and it led directly to the institutionalization of homosexuality as a sickness.

In the nineteenth century, then, when the first scientific discussions of homosexuality appear, it is not surprising that such behavior is seen as abnormal. When the American Psychiatric Association, beginning in 1952, created the Diagnostic and Statistical Manual of Mental Disorders (American Psychiatric Association, 1968), homosexuality was listed at the top of the list of sexual deviations (the other sexual deviations being fetishism, paedophilia, transvestitism, exhibitionism, and sadism and masochism). It was not until 1973, when, by a democratic vote by its members, the DSM removed homosexuality from its list of mental illnesses. Egodystonic homosexuality remained a DSM classification until 1986 when it was removed because it created more confusion than illumination (Bayer, 1987). Just as homosexuality became an illness without reference to (then non-existent) research, so too, it was removed without reference to existing literature.

The combination of the religious teachings about the nature of developing children's minds, and the popularization of the early theories of human psychological development, clearly established that children could be corrupted by immoral influences. As homosexuality was a crime, a developmental deviancy, and a moral failing in the eyes of the church, it therefore stood to reason that homosexuality posed a threat to children. No evidence was offered in support of these assumptions, but laws and implicit social policies were created to protect families and children from the influences of homosexuals. In fact, most researchers agree that a disproportionately high number of sexual offenses against children are committed by heterosexual men (Finkelhor, 1984).

Lesbian and gay youth are themselves at increased risk of various forms of abuse (Comstock, 1991; Harry, 1989; Savin-Williams, 1989). While the vast majority may not be identifiable to their parents and peers, the abuse of many who are identified or even suspected as homosexuals stands as a harsh reminder to others of the dangers of disclosure. Disclosure may jeopardize already tenuous family dynamics. Losses may include family support and peer affiliation (Borhek, 1988) with consequent isolation, emotional distress, economic vulnerability and associated health risks (Robertson, 1981), in addition to the loss of educational and employment opportunities (Remafedi, 1987). These losses are in the domains most central to the adolescent's preparation for adult life and may therefore constitute significant developmental impediments. In this context, it is not surprising that many sexual minority youth opt for denial or compartmentalization and that families collude consciously or unconsciously with that adaptation. Self-suppression and family denial complete an effective cycle of repression. The needs of a vulnerable population are submerged, prevailing social contradictions go unchecked, and the public policy void goes unchallenged. But neither psychological nor social repression is long endured without consequence, and positive adjustment among sexual minority youth is associated with disclosure, parental acceptance, and social support (Strommen, 1990). Repression, denial and ignorance do these youths no service, but are at the root of the difficulties sexual minority youth face.

Although it has been widely accepted within the social science community for many years that homosexuality is widespread

(Kinsey et al., 1948; Bell and Weinberg, 1978) and that gay people do not have a higher incidence of mental health problems than the general population (Hooker, 1957), the belief that it is somehow morally deviant has persisted. The vocal opposition of minority groups who belong to well-established and financially stable organizations (mostly affiliated with church groups), has blocked reform. One of the arguments used to deny gay people legal recognition as a minority group is based on the belief that gay people choose to be gay. Where there is choice, there is reason and responsibility, and therefore this belief rationalizes limited conceptions of homosexuality as sin. Whereas an immutable condition is something the individual cannot be held responsible for, a chosen course of action does not escape judgement. Some religions have attempted to deal with this by distinguishing the sin from the sinner. In other words, being homosexual does not automatically imperil the soul so long as the feelings are never acted on. In the secular domain, Reiter (1989) has addressed the question of choice by demonstrating the difference between sexual orientation and sexual identity. She argues that sexual orientation is not a choice, but that sexual identity (like behavior) derives from the interaction of choice and opportunity. Identity does not automatically follow behavior. For the adult, as for the adolescent, feelings may emerge but remain dissociated from identity. For that matter, feelings may not lead to behavior that gives rise to labelling by oneself or others. Conversely, a self-labelled homosexual may remain celibate while sustaining a homosexual identity based on recognition of the immutability of her/his feelings.

Researchers have not yet located a gay gene, but there is now evidence of a probable genetic factor in homosexuality (Buhrich, Bailey, and Martin, 1991). Other researchers have determined that variations in hormone levels during critical periods of uterine life can induce homosexual behaviour in animals and in humans (Dorner, 1988; Money, 1987). These, and other studies like them (Ehrhardt et al., 1985; Dahlgren et al., 1991), suggest that it is highly probable that homosexuality has a biological basis that interacts with the environment to influence the expression of homosexual inclinations and identities.

CONCLUSION

On the balance of existing evidence, it is not reasonable to conclude that sexual orientation is a choice. Arguments for unequal treatment based on the assumption of choice are therefore irreconcilable with both moral justice and competent practice in any of the disciplines that interact with public policy. Homophobia is intrinsically problematic. Homosexuality is not. The negative connotations associated with the latter are a social construction deriving from unnecessary consequences of stigmatization and demoralization. Advocacy must therefore be a part of ethical, responsible and effective social service planning for gay and lesbian youth. Where misinformation and sectarian moral conceptions are themselves the problem, they must be confronted as such and their influence put in a perspective that improves equity and increases the developmental prospects of a minority that has already given much evidence of resilience.

REFERENCES

American Psychiatric Association (1968). *Diagnostic and statistical manual of mental disorders*. Washington, DC. American Psychiatric Association.

Bayer, R. (1987). *Homosexuality and American psychiatry*. Princeton, NJ: Princeton University Press.

Bell, A. & Weinberg, M. (1978). *Homosexualities: A study of diversity among men and women*. New York: Simon & Schuster.

Borhek, M. (1988). Helping gay and lesbian adolescents and their families. *Journal of Adolescent Health Care, 9*(2), 123-128.

Boxer, A. & Cohler, B. (1989). The life course of gay and lesbian youth: An immodest proposal for the study of lives. In G. Herdt (Ed.), *Gay and Lesbian Youth*. New York: Harrington Park Press.

Buhrich, N., Bailey, J.M., & Martin, N.G. (1991). Sexual orientation, sexual identity, and sex-dimorphic behaviors in male twins. *Behavior Genetics, 21*(1), 75-96.

Cass, V. (1991). Homosexual identity formation: A theoretical model. *Journal of Homosexuality, 4*(3), 219-235.

Comstock, G. (1991). *Violence against lesbians and gay men*. New York: Columbia University Press.

Dahlgren, I.L., Matuszczyk, J.V., & Hard, E. (1991). Sexual orientation in male rats prenatally exposed to ethanol. *Neurotoxicology, 13*, 267-269.

Dorner, G. (1988). Neuroendocrine response to estrogen and brain differentiation in heterosexuals, homosexuals, and transexuals. *Archives of Sexual Behavior, 17*(1), 57-75.

Duberman, M., Vicinus, M., & Chauncey, G., Jr. (Eds.). (1989). *Hidden from history: Reclaiming the gay and lesbian past.* New York: Meridian-Penguin Books.

Ehrhardt, A.A., Meyer-Bahlburg, H.F.L., Rosen, L.R., Feldman, J.F., Veridiano, N.P., Zimmerman, I., & McEwen, B.S. (1985). Sexual orientation after prenatal exposure to exognous estrogen. *Archives of Sexual Behavior, 14*(1), 57-75.

Finkelhor, D. (1984). *Child sexual abuse.* New York: The Free Press.

Foucault, M. (1980). *The history of sexuality.* New York: Pantheon.

Gonsiorek, J.C. (1988). Mental health issues of gay and lesbian adolescents. *Journal of Adolescent Health Care, 9*(2), 114-122.

Harry, J. (1989). Parental physical abuse and sexual orientation in males. *Archives of Sexual Behavior, 18*(3), 251-261.

Herdt, G. (1989). Introduction: Gay and lesbian youth, emergent identities, and cultural scenes at home and abroad. In G. Herdt (Ed.), *Gay and lesbian youth.* New York: Harrington Park Press.

Hooker, E. (1957). The adjustment of the male overt homosexual. *Journal of Projective Techniques, 21*(18).

Kinsey, A.C., Pomeroy, W.B., & Martin, C.E. (1948). *Sexual behavior in the human male.* Philadelphia: W.B. Saunders.

Minton, H.L. & McDonald, G.J. (1984). Homosexual identity formation as a developmental process. *Journal of Homosexuality, 9*(4), 91-103.

Money, J. (1987). Sin, sickness, or status? Homosexual gender identity and psychoneuroendocrinology. *American Psychologist, 42*(4), 384-399.

Offer, D. & Sabshin, M. (Eds.). (1984). *Normality and the life cycle.* New York: Basic Books.

Powell, G., Yamamoto, J., Romero, A., & Morales, A. (Eds.). (1983). *The psychosocial development of minority group children.* New York: Brunner/Mazel.

Reiter, L. (1989). Sexual orientation, sexual identity, and the question of choice. *Clinical Social Work Journal, 17*(2), 138-150.

Remafedi, G. (1987). Adolescent homosexuality: Psychosocial and medical implications. *Pediatrics, 79,* 331-337.

Rivera, R.R. (1991). Sexual orientation and the law. In J. Gonsiorek & J. Weinrich (Eds.), *Homosexuality Research implications for public policy.* Newbury Park: Sage Publications, Inc.

Robertson, R. (1981). Young gays. In J. Hart & D. Richardson (Eds.), *The theory and practice of homosexuality.* London: Routledge and Kegan Paul.

Ross, M.W. (1989). Gay youth in four cultures: A comparative study. In G. Herdt, (Ed.), *Gay and lesbian youth.* New York: Harrington Park Press.

Savin-Williams, R.C. (1989). Parental influences on the self-esteem of gay and lesbian youths: A reflected appraisals model. In G. Herdt (Ed.), *Gay and lesbian youth.* New York: Harrington Park Press.

Strommen, E.F. (1990). Hidden branches and growing pains: Homosexuality and the family tree. In F.W. Bozett & M.B. Sussman (Eds.), *Homosexuality and family relations.* New York: Harrington Park Press.

Troiden, R. (1988). *Gay and lesbian identity: A sociological analysis.* Six Hills, NY: General Hall, Inc.

Service Organizations for Gay and Lesbian Youth

Greg Greeley

SUMMARY. This paper discusses six youth service organizations that represent different solutions to the same problem: the acceptance of sexual minority youth. These solutions include youth-led groups, organizations dedicated to training and education, and agencies that provide direct services to youth. This chapter tries to bring some insight into the forces that formed these groups and discusses some of the new directions in the youth service community. Although each of these groups started with different structures and services, many have evolved to offer a common set of services. Future organizations will be able to benefit from this by assembling programs from the model components that have already been implemented. Future work should enhance those effective service components that have received little attention and develop new models to meet youth needs.

INTRODUCTION

This article discusses six different organizations that provide services to gay, lesbian, bisexual and transgender youth. There are

Greg Greeley, MS, is a Washington, DC activist. He was a founder of the Sexual Minority Assistance League, and served as President of SMYAL's Board of Directors. In 1993, Greeley spearheaded the drive to empower sexual minority youth to participate in the Youth Empowerment Speakout at the National March on Washington for Lesbian, Gay, and Bisexual Rights.

[Haworth co-indexing entry note]: "Service Organizations for Gay and Lesbian Youth." Greeley, Greg. Co-published simultaneously in *Journal of Gay & Lesbian Social Services* (The Haworth Press, Inc.) Vol. 1, No. 3/4, 1994, pp. 111-130; and: *Helping Gay and Lesbian Youth: New Policies, New Programs, New Practice* (ed: Teresa DeCrescenzo) The Haworth Press, Inc., 1994, pp. 111-130. Multiple copies of this article/chapter may be purchased from The Haworth Document Delivery Center [1-800-3-HAWORTH; 9:00 a.m. - 5:00 p.m. (EST)].

over 150 organizations dedicated to sexual minority youth (Hetrick-Martin Institute, 1993). The organizations discussed here were selected because they each represent a different approach to the same problem: the acceptance of sexual minority youth. These approaches include youth-led groups, organizations dedicated to educating mainstream service providers about the needs of sexual minority youth, and agencies that provide direct services to youth.

This paper tries to bring some insight into the forces that formed these groups. More than ever before, it is important to understand why these groups were founded, and why they provide their particular services, so that the lessons of the past will not have to be re-learned by future services providers and community organizers. Ten years ago, there were fewer than a dozen groups dedicated to helping lesbian and gay youth. In looking at the history of youth service in Boston, for example, it is clear that organizations that do not listen to their youth will fail. Experiences in other cities have shown that adult volunteers, however well intentioned, are not equipped to provide youth services without professional direction.

This paper also discusses some of the future directions for the youth service community. Because this movement is so young, experimental and pilot programs will likely play a major role in expanding the set of model programs that new organizations will emulate in the future.

BOSTON ALLIANCE OF GAY AND LESBIAN YOUTH

Boston Alliance of Gay and Lesbian Youth (BAGLY) is a youth-run social support group for lesbian, gay and bisexual youth. Support groups include meetings for new members, separate men's and women's groups, and general meetings. Sunday afternoons are informal drop-in days for socializing. BAGLY also offers a peer counseling program. The toll-free hotline provides referrals, listings of upcoming events, women's information, AIDS information and referrals to local groups and services for youth.

Boston had substantial gay youth activity before BAGLY. In the early 70s, the Homophile Union of Boston sponsored the Boston Gay Youth, an adult run group for gay youth. By the mid 1970s, an informal gay community center had formed around the Charles

Street Meeting House, a Unitarian church. This center sponsored a gay youth group called Project Lambda that lasted until 1977. Finally, in the late 1970s, a group of gay activists formed the Committee for Gay Youth (CGY), an outgrowth of the adult gay organizations in the community, that sponsored a weekly youth rap group. These programs were run by volunteers with no professional direction.

In the spring of 1980, CGY experienced a "philosophical split" between the youth and the adults. The youth had put in a lot of work for a particular fund-raiser, and the adults didn't agree with the youth about how the money should be spent. This disagreement led several of the youth to formally incorporate as BAGLY and move into their own office on Tremont Street. CGY soon ceased to exist as an organization. The adults' failure to involve the youths had ramifications beyond CGY's demise as an organization. This failure prevented the adult lesbian and gay community in Boston from providing any significant youth services for almost a decade.

BAGLY's first year was exciting. The youth had their own space, and it was in use almost every day of the week. The core of youth who started BAGLY spent most of their time at the office, and it was a very empowering experience. There were two adult advisors, both of whom were in their early twenties. There was little other adult support. Within the adult lesbian and gay community, BAGLY had some visibility but minimal financial support; it was clearly a youth run organization.

Unfortunately, BAGLY could not afford the rent for their office past the first year. Moving out of the Tremont Street space forced BAGLY into a transition. It eventually relocated in St. John's Church. This relocation meant that BAGLY did not have a full time meeting space, and programs had to be curtailed. The lack of a full time space also changed the character of the youth coming to BAGLY. There were more suburban youth from family settings and fewer street and throwaway youth.

The next several years were a period of stabilization and measured growth for the youth at BAGLY. They developed programs for raising funds and began writing grants, public speaking, and reaching out to the media, and began advertising through public service announcements. In 1986, the youth formed an Adult Advisory Board to facilitate adult involvement and bring in more support from the community. In the late 1980s, BAGLY started to expand their programs. They added a peer-counseling program to formalize some of the relationships and support that already existed among the youth, and they received funding from the AIDS Action Council for HIV education.

Finally, however, the youth realized that there was more to do for youth than they could do alone. In 1992, the youth asked the Adult Advisory Board to form an organization to provide social services to lesbian and gay youth. This organization, Proud, was incorporated in 1993 and is composed of three programs: BAGLY, Home Base, and Youth Works. Home Base is planned as an emergency and transitional shelter for lesbian and gay youth. Youth Works is a set of services to help youth with career counseling, GED mentoring, and life skills.

GAY AND LESBIAN ADOLESCENT SOCIAL SERVICES (LOS ANGELES)

Gay and Lesbian Adolescent Social Services (GLASS) provides group homes for gay, lesbian, bisexual, transgendered, transvestite, and HIV-positive adolescents. GLASS is also a licensed foster family agency for gay and lesbian teens as well as for infants, toddlers and young children who have been abandoned, abused, or neglected. GLASS operates a school, in partnership with the Los Angeles Unified School District; conducts an intensive case management project for teens at high risk for HIV infection; offers mentoring to young gays and lesbians through its "paradigm project"; provides advanced college placement and scholarships to academically gifted gay and lesbian youth; and has designed a Single Room Occupancy residence program for young adult graduates of the GLASS residential programs.

GLASS was founded in 1984 by Teresa DeCrescenzo, whose 15 years as a social worker in the residential placement field gave her a first hand knowledge of the homophobic and overtly hostile rejection lesbian and gay youth received from the juvenile justice and social service systems. Many agencies would purposely exclude gay and lesbian youth from their programs. As a result, gay youth all too often were placed in lock up style facilities because no one else would accept them.

DeCrescenzo called this the "AHHH Syndrome" because agencies in the mid 1970s would use "Arson, Homicide, Heroin Addiction, and Homosexuality" collectively (as if they were all "equal") as reasons to exclude youth from their programs.

In 1985, shortly after incorporation as a city, the West Hollywood City Council voted to grant GLASS start-up funding for a six-bed, licensed group home. West Hollywood residents were concerned about street prostitution, petty theft, and the general appearance of its neighborhoods. An openly lesbian mayor who was very concerned about the needs of youth, and an openly gay city councilman helped secure $55,000 in city funds.

Financing was difficult during the first years at GLASS. When the first home opened, there was no money for staff and programs. All the money, plus an additional $100,000, borrowed at high interest, short term rates, had gone into the purchase of the home. In addition, there was a negative reaction from some parts of the community. A public campaign to oust several city council members in West Hollywood used GLASS funding as an issue. Those politicians who had arranged for the GLASS seed money from West Hollywood were coming under fire for their support. GLASS survived, however, in part because there was a large demand for its services. In 1979, Jerry Brown, then Governor of California, had signed an executive order preventing social service agencies from denying services to lesbian and gay youth. Because of this, agencies were searching for any way they could easily handle these youth. GLASS provided that service.

By 1987, there was such a demand for group home placement for lesbian and gay youth that the Los Angeles County Probation Department approached GLASS with $45,000 in seed money and asked the organization to open a second six bed facility. The Probation Department needed the spaces, and GLASS had already developed a solid reputation within the social service community. At the same time, another trend became apparent, that of HIV infection among youth. This trend lead GLASS to add services to minors with HIV infection, or minors at high risk for HIV infection, to its mission statement, thus adding another subpopulation to its client base. At the time, HIV was perceived in the social service community as a "gay problem." Currently, the majority of HIV positive youth living in GLASS group homes self identify as heterosexual.

A waiting list that consistently held six to ten youth convinced GLASS that a third home was needed. High interest rates and a huge debt load, however, kept GLASS near foreclosure and prevented any expansion. It took considerable lobbying and political maneuvering for GLASS to finally secure a refinancing package led by the Los Angeles Community Redevelopment Agency. The refinancing reduced the interest costs to GLASS, as well as the size of the house payments, thus allowing for the organization to open its third house in 1989, bringing the total number of beds to 18. (See elsewhere in this volume for Taylor's discussion of the social policy and lobbying issues, as well as the importance of coalitions with mainstream heterosexual institutions, which can assist in permitting a small, community-based, grass roots organization like GLASS to move its agenda forward.)

In 1989, GLASS expanded its mission to include foster care. GLASS recruited, screened, trained, certified, hired, and supervised lesbians and gays as foster parents. Once these foster parents were certified by GLASS, the county agencies began to refer children, infants through adolescents, in need of foster care to GLASS. The agency is responsible for all case management and psychosocial services, as well as the foster care placement itself, and is funded for this service through a system based on the age of the child and any special needs the child may have. At any one time, GLASS has approximately thirty youth in the group homes program, forty in the intensive case management HIV project, and forty in the foster home program.

The agency expanded to thirty group home beds by doubling the bed capacity of an existing home and adding a fourth house. In 1992, GLASS started a three-year trial program, funded by the Ryan White CARE Act, to provide intensive case management for medical services to at-risk youth. GLASS also opened the Eagle Center, an off-site branch of the Los Angeles Unified School District, as an alternative school for lesbian and gay youth.

GLASS is planning additional programmatic enhancements and bed expansion to meet the increasing demand for services.

THE HETRICK-MARTIN INSTITUTE (NEW YORK CITY)

The Hetrick-Martin Institute is a social service, education and advocacy agency for lesbian, gay, bisexual and homeless youth. Services include: individual, group and family counseling; training and resources for youth and professionals; referrals to medical, legal, employment and shelter services; an after-school drop-in center; HIV/AIDS services and education; the alternative Harvey Milk School; Project First Step program for homeless youth; and national advocacy.

The Hetrick-Martin Institute was founded in 1979, as the Institute for the Protection of Lesbian and Gay Youth by Emery Hetrick and Damien Martin. Hetrick and Martin were outraged by several tragic incidents involving gay youth in New York and wanted the Institute to advocate on behalf of these youth. (In one incident, a gay youth was gang raped in a shelter's shower. When the agency investigated the incident, it blamed the gay youth for what happened and kicked him out of the facility.) In New York, as in several other cities, there already was a youth service organization, Gay and Young, that sponsored youth groups. However, Gay and Young was lead by volunteers with no professional support and, because of this, eventually folded.

When the Institute started, it provided training and education as well as policy advocacy. The issue of providing direct services was controversial among the leadership because there was no general agreement on the overall direction of the Institute's programs. Some wanted to remain a training and education based organization that advocated on behalf of youth using a clinical model, while others felt that the Institute should reduce the boundaries that exist between youths and adults. Ultimately, those who advocated for a more clinical model prevailed.

The turning point for the Institute was the first Gay and Lesbian Health Conference in 1982. The research presented at this conference clearly indicated the need for services for lesbian and gay youth, and convinced the Institute that services should be a component of their programs. An anonymous gift and a matching grant from the New York City Youth Bureau allowed the Institute to hire a three member staff and open an office in late 1982. The Institute offered counseling and case management as its first direct service programs. The number of referrals was huge, and more than 500 youth were handled by the Institute in the first year.

In 1983, the Institute recognized the impending problem with AIDS and added an AIDS training program. That year also saw the Institute add a volunteer staff that ran a drop-in center and socialization groups for the youth. By 1985, the Institute was servicing over 1000 youth per year (excluding telephone assistance). Unfortunately, the Institute was virtually unnoticed in the lesbian and gay community. There was some support from individuals, but almost no coverage in the gay press.

This changed in 1985, when the Institute opened the Harvey Milk High School, an alternative school for lesbian and gay students. This gathered wide notice in the mainstream press, including editorial support from the New York Times. The Harvey Milk School marked a turning point for the Institute's visibility within the lesbian and gay community in New York. Since the mid 1980s, the Institute has continued to expand the scope of its programs, adding a Peer Education program, where lesbian and gay youth reach out to mainstream youth and youth service providers, and a Peer Mentoring program, which affords youth the chance to work as interns in gay or gay-positive environments.

The Hetrick-Martin Institute is moving in a new direction that other programs will likely emulate, that of youth leadership. The Institute has started a new peer intake process where youth, rather than adults, greet new youth. Youth who participate in the Institute's programs are no longer considered clients, but instead are "members," complete with membership cards. The Institute is also pressing for more access and education within mainstream organizations and individual families. The belief is that, where possible, gaining acceptance for young lesbians and gays in their families and their communities can greatly enhance their chances for success.

THE LOS ANGELES GAY AND LESBIAN COMMUNITY SERVICES CENTER

The Youth Services Department of the Los Angeles Gay and Lesbian Community Services Center provides a wide range of services to youth. The Outreach Project provides service information and referrals, material assistance, life stabilization, and medical assistance. The Center also provides a Youth Talkline, a Pen Pal Program, and a Youth Rap Group. The core of the Youth Services Program, however, is the Kruks/Tilsner Youth Shelter, a 24-bed transitional living program for runaway, homeless and throwaway youth. The program is designed as an intensive independent living program where youth can develop life skills necessary to become productive members of society.

The Center started providing services to youth in 1976 as part of their Prison, Probation and Parole Program. This program was run by two ex-offenders and was designed to provide advocacy on behalf of currently incarcerated offenders as well as services to those who had been recently paroled. It turned out that the bulk of the people assisted by this program were young hustlers, most under the age of 23, who were stuck in a revolving door between life on the street and life in jail. Although not necessarily gay, these youth were homeless and needed services. Recognizing this, the program was eventually renamed the Systems Assistance Program. Its main focus was to ensure the provision of services such as food stamps, welfare and housing to those in need.

In the late 1970s, the City of Los Angeles gave an empty home on Citrus Street to the Center to use as an emergency shelter. The Citrus House was originally run on a shoe string. It accepted the first eight comers, no age limit, who were allowed to "crash" there unsupervised for the evening. In the early 1980s, the focus shifted to youth, although there was still minimal supervision. This shift in focus was recognized by a new program name: Youth Services.

The Citrus House played a pivotal role in the Center's youth programs. At the time Citrus House was started, most gay identified youth did not feel comfortable in homeless shelters. These shelters were usually run by missions and would routinely kick out lesbian and gay youth. The typical youth client used sex for survival and did not fit the mold expected by many skid-row missions. In addition, most gay youth didn't fit the mold of runaway shelters. The emphasis in runaway shelters in the early 1980s was to reunite the family. Shelters were frequently required to call parents within 24 hours and youth were limited to a two week stay. Unfortunately, most youth in Los Angeles either had no family or had been kicked out of, rather than run away from, their homes.

The experience at the Center was that roughly a third of the youth on the street were gay identified, and many of them came from other cities or states. Because the existing runaway shelters were geared towards reunification, they were ineffective. It was difficult to refer these gay youth to a shelter, because there was usually no hope for reunification and the youth would be back out in the street in two weeks. Most youth had been through the system and it had failed them. This service gap only made the youth's situation worse because this system failure made the youth believe that they had failed.

In the mid 80s, the Children's Hospital in Los Angeles took the lead in forming "Project Homeless Youth." The hospital found that street youth would use small medical problems as an excuse to come into the emergency room for free care. Children's Hospital designed a "user friendly" intake process for street youth that went beyond the immediate symptoms and did a true needs assessment for the youth. The Project Homeless Youth network eventually became a well-designed agency network for matching youth with service providers. The result was that each service provider functioned as an intake point for all the other members of the consortium. Thus, if a gay youth in need of housing appeared at the LA Free Clinic, that youth would be referred to the Center. The network also improved relations with the police, because they could bring a youth to any member agency and the youth would be cared for. Previously, a homeless youth meant the officer had to complete paper work, set the youth up in a foster home, locate the youth's family, and arrange for a bus ticket home. Often, the same youth would reappear. The support from the police was important because their fear was that opening up youth shelters in Hollywood would simply attract more youth to the area. The result, in fact, was the opposite, and there were fewer youth on the streets after the shelters opened.

In the late 1980s, the years of effort spent convincing organizations on a national level of the need for transitional living facilities paid off. The Center received a large, five-year grant from the Department of Housing and Urban Development to fund the Citrus

House. This influx of money allowed the Center to greatly expand the services offered by the shelter. The average youth stay was increased from two weeks to three months, the number of staff members increased, and the shelter was able to offer additional programs for youth.

Other changes have been dramatic. The Citrus House, now renamed the Kruks/Tilsner Youth Shelter, has made the transition from a short-term drop-in shelter with a small staff, to a full service transitional living facility with a staff firmly rooted in the mental health profession. Youth in the facility have five different case management tracks available to help them build the life skills necessary to become productive members of society. The Center hopes to expand their service offerings to include a 24-hour drop-in program and an independent living program that would allow youth to live on their own in an apartment-style facility without giving up the case management and support from the Center.

PROJECT 10 (LOS ANGELES)

Project 10 is an on-campus high-school counseling program founded in 1984 by Dr. Virginia Uribe, and is committed to keeping students in school, off drugs and sexually responsible. The services of Project 10 include workshops and training sessions for administrators and staff personnel, informal drop-in counseling, outreach to parents, liaison with peer counseling, substance abuse and suicide prevention programs, and coordination with health education programs that encourage sexual responsibility.

Before Project 10 existed, nothing was being done in the Los Angeles school system for lesbian and gay youth. Surveys painted a terrible picture of the environment there. Eventually it was rage that drove Uribe to start Project 10. At Fairfax High School, where she worked, a young gay "throwaway" youth was driven out of school. The student had been transferred to Fairfax from another school. At Fairfax, he was physically abused by peers and verbally abused by both peers and adults. He finally dropped out of school entirely and turned to the streets. His experience at Fairfax was simply a repeat of the experience that he had at his previous four schools. He had been submitted to so much obvious abuse that there was a letter in his file from the Gay and Lesbian Community Services Center registering a complaint about "gay bashing."

After seeing firsthand the treatment that openly gay students received in her school, Uribe decided to act. She approached a group of lesbian and gay students and proposed that they meet on a regular basis. The youth agreed to come, although at first they didn't understand "why anyone would care" about them. Uribe came out to the students to help build their trust in her. The group eventually peaked at nearly 25 students. Within this group, Uribe found many bright youth who unfortunately had many problems. Most were alienated and felt unaccepted.

Once the group started, Uribe went to the Principal of Fairfax High. He was supportive and asked her to develop a pilot program. She solicited involvement from the Board of Education to protect the program's future potential. Project 10 developed along four lines: Education, Support, Information and Safety.

The education component started as mandatory workshops for counselors and faculty, then continued as voluntary inservice sessions. These workshops and inservice sessions were designed to educate and sensitize the adults at Fairfax about how to deal with lesbian and gay youth. The reaction from most of the faculty was supportive; a few were indifferent; none were openly hostile. Most, however, felt awkward about the subject of lesbian and gay students.

The support component began with the informal rap group already underway. The students involved with the group were at first surprised that the school would even sponsor such a thing. It worked, however, and the students thought the group was wonderful, their attendance improved, and it sent them a very positive message.

The information component started as a library project. The goal was to ensure that the Fairfax library had gay positive books. These books were both fiction and non-fiction that dealt with subjects like parents, religion, and AIDS.

Finally, the safety component was based on developing a code of conduct for students and faculty at Fairfax to ensure that openly lesbian and gay students felt safe. Overall, Project 10 opened the discussion of lesbian and gay youth in education circles. Hundreds of requests came in for information and it was clear that the subject was out of the closet. The education system finally recognized that lesbian and gay students exist and that something needed to be done to ensure that they had a safe and secure education environment.

Over the next several years, the Board of Education gave Uribe a half day of non-class time to expand Project 10 to the rest of the secondary schools in the Los Angeles Unified School District. Despite some publicity, there was no organized opposition. Dr. Uribe met with principals, counselors and faculty from many of the system's schools. She also targeted nurses and psychologists within the system with a massive educational campaign. The harassment code at Fairfax had not yet been adopted by other schools, but there was a change in attitude. There was even a case of a student being transferred out of a school for harassing another student and using the word "faggot." This expansion culminated in the formation of Friends of Project 10 in 1987. Friends of Project 10 started because people wanted to donate money to the project, and there was no place for it to go except the school system. The Friends of Project 10 has grown to several thousand donors who help pay for scholarships, educational materials and videos for Project 10.

In 1988, Project 10 came to a conservative school within the Los Angeles district. A California Assemblywoman heard about a speech at the school, and targeted Project 10. She joined forces with Rev. Lou Sheldon and the Traditional Values Coalition to introduce a resolution in the California State Assembly to force Los Angeles to drop Project 10 or lose all state funding. There was a large amount of publicity, and the Los Angeles Times gave strong editorial support for Project 10. The result was a day-long hearing at the Board of Education. Good organizing on behalf of Project 10 lead to a successful hearing and the Board re-affirmed its support of the program. That year, the school district implemented a system-wide harassment code.

In 1991, the Los Angeles Unified School District took the next step by forming a Gay and Lesbian Education Commission. The Commission has a Director and a volunteer staff who monitor conditions for lesbian and gay youth and make recommendations to the Board of Education on lesbian and gay youth issues.

Project 10 also completed a Library Project dedicated to placing gay-positive books from the Parents and Friends of Lesbians and Gays reading list in all secondary school libraries in Los Angeles.

THE SEXUAL MINORITY YOUTH ASSISTANCE LEAGUE (WASHINGTON, D.C.)

The Sexual Minority Youth Assistance League (SMYAL) is the primary agency in the Washington, DC area dealing with youth who are lesbian, gay, bisexual or transgender. SMYAL services include facilitated youth groups, a drop-in program, a help line, a speakers' bureau, a counselor training program, a peer to peer HIV education program, and various advertising and education campaigns for suicide prevention and general awareness of lesbian and gay issues.

SMYAL started in 1984, when several area counselors and social workers called a conference to discuss services provided to sexual minority youth. At its inception, SMYAL was an organization dedicated to training and education. The Board of Directors believed that the best way to serve sexual minority youth was to educate youth service providers, rather than to provide services itself. There were several factors that lead to this decision. The SMYAL leadership was primarily composed of activists from the lesbian and gay community, not professionals from the youth service community. Thus, the role of training and education was more familiar than the role of providing direct service to youth.

Another factor was a previous volunteer-based youth group that was active in Washington during the late 1970s and early 1980s. This group ran into difficulties in determining what boundaries were appropriate between the adult group leaders and the youth. These difficulties eventually lead to the breakup of the group and certainly contributed to SMYAL's decision to concentrate solely on training and education.

During SMYAL's early years, it was clear that training and education were very much in need. The District of Columbia was not well equipped to handle the sexual minority youth within its social service system. Youth caught kissing in a car were faced with criminal prosecution, transgender and cross-dressing youth were incarcerated in St. Elizabeth's Psychiatric Hospital, and youth who were HIV positive had their status treated with less confidentiality than a routine medical examination.

While SMYAL as an organization was limited to training and education, individual leaders voluntarily took on intervention and advocacy on behalf of individual youth in crisis. After seeing the difficulties these youth faced, it became clear that the single biggest gap in the services provided to sexual minority youth was the lack of peer affiliation. Starting a peer socialization group was viewed as a relatively easy way to fill that service gap. In 1987, SMYAL organized a program for recruiting and training volunteers to facilitate a youth group. SMYAL training included the theory behind the importance of socialization (using the Erik Erickson model of adolescent development) as well as a strong professional direction. In addition, SMYAL set a firm boundary for the adults in how they deal with the youth. This was important not only to provide appropriate service to the youth, but to avoid repeating the problems experienced with the District's original youth group.

Having a strong theoretical underpinning and professional direction for the youth group paid off in two ways. Most of the youth served by the program had no issues other than their sexual orientation. However, when youth with bigger problems came along, it was relatively easy for facilitators to spot those problems and refer these youth to the appropriate professional organizations. The second advantage of the professional direction was in persuading professionals to refer their clients to SMYAL. Eventually, therapists started referring their youth to SMYAL saying, "You don't need therapy, you need SMYAL."

Today, SMYAL is still known for its training and education programs. It has programs for suicide prevention, using a poster advertising campaign; and counselor training, for guidance counselors and other adults who have routine contact with youth. In addition, Project Lifeguard provides a peer to peer education program for HIV prevention. SMYAL has expanded its youth groups to include a drop-in center on Friday and Sunday in addition to the regular Saturday sessions. Finally, SMYAL has added a help line for youth that is operated Monday through Friday evenings. For future programs, SMYAL has started to investigate how to add case management, counseling and housing to its services.

NEW INITIATIVES

The community of organizations serving sexual minority youth has grown dramatically since the early 1980s. What started out as a quiet movement that received little attention from both the gay and mainstream society, has become a leading indicator of the maturity of the lesbian and gay community.

Much of the growth in the next decade will be in new services. Experimental programs and pilot initiatives are the keys to developing these services. An excellent example of these new initiatives is the Foster Care Program of the Gay and Lesbian Community Center of Colorado. This program provides housing for lesbian and gay youth from 18 to 20 who are no longer eligible for state sponsored foster care. Adult volunteers are trained by the state as foster parents, and the Community Center calls on the volunteers as housing is needed. By doing this, the Community Center can provide housing to these youth without the huge expense of operating a shelter. Had the Community Center simply tried to use existing programs as models, they would not be sheltering youth today. It is important to communicate these successes to other service providers on a national level.

The key to communication on a national level started with the American Friends Service Committee (AFSC) Bridges Project. The Bridges Project was founded in 1992, to develop a national network of organizations serving sexual minority youth and to inspire youth serving agencies to include and support sexual minority youth in their programs. The first major event sponsored by the Bridges Project was the Youth Empowerment Speakout (YES) at the 1993 March on Washington. The goals of YES were to provide a safe environment for youth, and for youth service providers to exchange information and experiences. The service providers' role was to offer assistance in planning and documenting the sexual minority youth forum. The youth role was to determine the agenda and discuss their needs and desires.

The outgrowth of the Bridges Project is the National Coalition for Youth and Sexual Orientation, which was founded in April, 1993. This organization already includes many of the large organizations active in the sexual minority youth community and will hopefully expand to include all interested organizations. The National

Coalition has several goals, including: coordinate the sharing of programs, resources, and information among service providers; facilitate communication and organization among our community's youth on a national level; and develop a National Policy and Legislative Strategy for youth and sexual orientation.

CONCLUSIONS

Each of the six organizations discussed here was started by people trying to solve specific problems. BAGLY started as a youth-led group; Hetrick-Martin, SMYAL and Project 10 as training and education organizations; the Center's Youth Services as a case management system; and GLASS as a group home. Because of this, the services offered by each of these organizations were different. Over the past decade, however, many of these groups have gradually evolved to offer a common set of services. These services can be broken into five major categories: Training and Education, Youth Groups, Housing, Case Management, and Counseling.

Training and Education covers a broad range of programs from general public awareness to seminars for professional service providers to youth HIV education. While some organizations were solely dedicated to training and education, all the organizations discussed here have found that training and education in some form have become an integral part of their service offerings.

Youth Groups, whether they are led by youth, volunteers or professionals, have become another fixture in all six groups discussed here. These groups are excellent vehicles to provide youth with the chance to develop their peer affiliation and reduce their feelings of loneliness and isolation. Especially with those youth whose major issue is sexual orientation, the youth groups allow them to work through their feelings and come to a resolution of their identities.

Although housing for youth is currently provided by only two of the six organizations (GLCSC and GLASS), SMYAL and BAGLY have both identified housing as a service component to be provided in the future. The programs at GLASS and GLCSC present two clear models for emulation, one of group and foster homes for youth under 18 who are not yet emancipated, and transitional living shelter for emancipated youth.

Case management goes hand in hand with housing, and it is often used as a precursor to offering shelter. Both GLASS and GLCSC have case management components as a part of their housing programs. In addition, those organizations which have identified an interest in housing have included case management as a part of their housing programs. The case management programs generally include service access and evaluation for both internally and externally supplied services. At SMYAL, case management was identified as a means of identifying shortcomings in existing services, and determining which new services to offer in the future.

Counseling programs vary widely. In some cases, such as BAGLY, peer-counseling for youths is provided. In other cases, counseling is done professionally and even includes families. Part of the reason counseling programs vary is that they are available from a wide variety of sources, not just the lesbian and gay community. In addition, because professional counseling is expensive on a per client basis, funding comprehensive programs is difficult.

In the past, sexual minority youth organizations were founded to combat specific problems. They were forced to develop from the ground up, in isolation, because there were few models, and little communication among organizations. As we have seen, organizations have started to converge in the services that they offer. Future organizations will be able to benefit by modeling the work already done in the field. Each community has different needs; therefore, no single model program could work for everyone. However, an organization dedicated to serving sexual minority youth can put together a solid set of services by assembling programs from the model components that have already been implemented.

Although the program components discussed above provide a wide range of necessary services to youth, there are two components that have not received as much attention as they might: youth empowerment and youth advocacy. With the exception of BAGLY, which is youth led, the youth programs here generally use clinical models for their work. As more youth come out, possibly at younger ages, there will be an increasing need for youth-led programs that "empower" youth to develop and take charge of their destiny. The Youth Empowerment Speakout held during the March on Washington in 1993 is an example of this movement. Youth set the agenda, ran the event, and created a safe space to network and organize without extensive adult direction.

The other area for future growth, advocacy and lobbying on behalf of youth issues, is an area that service providers have traditionally avoided. Direct lobbying and policy advocacy are not generally viewed as the role of service providers. There has been little activity in this area from the lesbian and gay lobbying organizations. If this continues, youth service providers will eventually have to fill this role as well. To date, the Hetrick-Martin Institute has generally taken a lead on this issue. Most work on the national level, however, will probably be done with the newly formed National Coalition for Youth and Sexual Orientation.

Overall, the lesbian and gay youth movement appears poised for growth. There is a subtle irony in the fact that, after working so hard to convince the youth service community that reunification with the family was not the only answer to helping homeless and runaway youth, the lesbian and gay youth community has come to the realization that the family may actually be a powerful tool in helping youth. The last decade was a time for trail blazers and new programs. Our next decade will be filled with a set of solid programs and a rapid expansion in the number of organizations involved in the movement.

REFERENCE

Hetrick-Martin Institute. (1993). *You are not alone*. National Lesbian, Gay and Bisexual Youth Organization Directory. New York.

ORGANIZATIONS

Bridges Project of American Friends Service Committee
National Coalition for Youth and Sexual Orientation
1501 Cherry Street
Philadelphia, PA 19102. (215) 741-7000

Boston Alliance of Gay and Lesbian Youth (BAGLY)
P.O. Box 814
Boston, MA 02103. (800) 42-BAGLY

Gay and Lesbian Community Center
P.O. Drawer E
Denver, CO 80218. (303) 831-6268

Gay and Lesbian Adolescent Social Services (GLASS)
650 North Robertson Blvd., Suite A
West Hollywood, CA 90069-5022. (310) 358-8727

The Hetrick-Martin Institute
401 West Street
New York, NY 10014. (212) 633-8920

Los Angeles Gay and Lesbian Community Services Center
1625 North Hudson Avenue
Los Angeles, CA 90028. (213) 993-7400

Project 10
7850 Melrose Ave
Los Angeles, CA 90046. (213) 651-5200

Sexual Minority Youth Assistance League (SMYAL)
333 1/2 Pennsylvania Avenue SE, 3rd floor
Washington, DC 20003. (202) 546-5940

HIV Risk in Gay and Lesbian Adolescents

William B. Pederson

SUMMARY. Adolescents, regardless of sexual orientation, are at increased risk for HIV infection. Although the number of infected adolescents remains small, the number of adolescent AIDS cases is approximately doubling each year. This suggests that the rate of HIV infection among adolescents is expanding in a similar fashion to that seen among gay men in the early years of the epidemic. The purpose of this paper is to provide a framework for understanding the problem of HIV infection as it relates to the gay and lesbian adolescent. This framework is grounded in developmental theory, though key social, political, economic, and policy factors which are believed to contribute to the infection of HIV among gay and lesbian adolescents will also be presented. It will be argued that social practitioners who are working in the HIV and AIDS arena would do well to reexamine the paradigm which governs existing practice methodology.

HIV INFECTION AMONG ADOLESCENTS

The pattern of HIV infection among adolescents remains relatively unknown, and culling this information is difficult. "To date, national seroprevalence data (among adolescents) have been reported on military recruits, Job Corp entrants, patients treated in sexually transmitted disease (STD) clinics, and homeless and runaway youth"

William B. Pederson, MSW, is a social worker and program consultant in Los Angeles, currently completing doctoral studies at the University of Southern California, School of Social Work.

[Haworth co-indexing entry note]: "HIV Risk in Gay and Lesbian Adolescents." Pederson, William B. Co-published simultaneously in *Journal of Gay & Lesbian Social Services* (The Haworth Press, Inc.) Vol. 1, No. 3/4, 1994, pp. 131-147; and: *Helping Gay and Lesbian Youth: New Policies, New Programs, New Practice* (ed: Teresa DeCrescenzo) The Haworth Press, Inc., 1994, pp. 131-147. Multiple copies of this article/chapter may be purchased from The Haworth Document Delivery Center [1-800-3-HA-WORTH; 9:00 a.m. - 5:00 p.m. (EST)].

131

(Boyer and Kegeles, 1991). The rates of HIV infection in those youth applying for military service nationally were 0.32 per 1,000 in women and 0.35 per 1,000 in men. Furthermore of those youth tested by the Job Corps between 1987 and 1990, the rates of HIV infection were 3.7 per 1,000 in men and 3.2 per 1,000 in women. Los Angeles County collected blind blood samples between 1990 and 1992, from clients 13 through 24 years of age, who were seen at selected sexually transmitted disease and family planning clinics, and tested them for HIV. From the samples collected, 225 positive tests were found, with an overall seroprevalence rate of 10.9 per 1,000 (Los Angeles County Adolescent HIV Consortium, 1993).

The assertion that a new wave of the AIDS epidemic is beginning to move into the adolescent population becomes more compelling when the number of AIDS cases in the 20-29 year age group is examined. As of September 30, 1993, there were 63,718 reported cases of AIDS among this age group, with 12,712 cases in the 20-24 year age group, and 51,006 cases in the 25-29 year age group (The Centers for Disease Control, 1993). Furthermore, it has been reported that one-fifth, or 20% of all AIDS cases in the United States, have been in the 20-29 year age group (Hingson et al., 1990). Given the incubation period of as much as eight or nine years between HIV seroconversion and the onset of the first symptoms of AIDS, it seems reasonable, even conservative, to infer that the majority of these individuals were infected as adolescents (Hingson, 1990; Needle et al., 1989; Naughton et al., 1991).

The American medical establishment, the scientific community, politicians, and society in general approached the problem of HIV infection with shortsighted vision, implementing social, political and economic sanctions that were grounded in homophobia. The notion existed that HIV infection was unique to one's group affiliation, and would be contained within those "marginalized" populations. This notion ignores two critical concepts. First, regardless of group affiliation, the ease of global travel and the multinational nature of modern business connections alone preclude the notion that HIV infection can be contained within specific groups. Second, the developmental tasks inherent in adolescence automatically increase the risk for HIV infection, regardless of sexual orientation.

This is particularly evident when one examines the manner in which adolescents attempt to master the tasks unique to their developmental life stage.

THE DEVELOPMENTAL LIFE STAGE OF ADOLESCENCE

Erickson's (1963) work on ego development as the mastery of stage-specific developmental tasks and crises provides a framework for understanding adolescent development. He argues that the time period of adolescence serves as an opportunity for one to integrate past, present and future interactions into a whole which represents one's unique self. Consolidation of this identity involves: time, self-certainty, role experimentation, anticipation of achievement, sexual identity, acceptance of leadership, and commitment to basic values (Goldstein, 1984).

Erickson's notion of ego identity is especially poignant, when considered in this context, in that two overriding issues emerge for the adolescent struggling with a gay or lesbian identity. First, sexual identity formation, regardless of sexual orientation, is a life task that all adolescents are challenged to accomplish. Therefore, it can be assumed that adolescents will seek out opportunity with members of either gender, in order to consolidate this aspect of their identity. Consequently, the adolescent *must* engage in extensive experimental sexual behavior to learn the roles and experiences congruent with innate capacities (Malyon, 1981). Young people are having both heterosexual and homosexual experiences, irrespective of what we might wish for them by way of abstinence or even caution. One has only to examine current pregnancy and STD rates among adolescents to substantiate this assertion.

Erickson's concept of ego identity assumes that the environment will provide opportunity for adolescents to consolidate their sexual identity into their whole self. These environmental opportunities are unavailable in an ideal form for the gay or lesbian adolescent, due to the prejudices inherent in the notion of homophobia (Malyon, 1981; Slater, 1988; Martin & Hetrick, 1988; Bidwell, 1988; Gonsiorek, 1988; Mercier & Berger, 1989; Martin, 1982; Minton & McDonald, 1984). When internal (little sense of competence) and external resources are insufficient or unavailable, the gay or lesbian adolescent will experience role confusion which will contribute to frustration and low self-esteem. According to Goldstein (1984): " . . . adolescents who suffer from role confusion often may adopt dysfunctional or antisocial behavior as a way of achieving some type of identity, even a negative one, that is, an identity considered undesirable by one's family or by society." Sexual acting out, prostitution, drug and alcohol abuse, suicide attempts, and school failure are all examples of behaviors seen among gay and lesbian adolescents struggling with their role in the context of a hostile environment.

Examination of environmental barriers to achieving consolidation of a positive gay or lesbian sexual identity may require a framework different from that which has been provided by the Ericksonian model. While acknowledging that identity is a relevant issue of adolescence, Offer and Sabshin (1984) argue that, by focusing on studies of the self as a central psychological issue crucial to normal adolescent development, rather than identity, the major psychological aspects of the adolescent period can be demonstrated. Offer and Sabshin examine five psychosocial areas of adolescence that are significant contributing factors to adjustment. These psychosocial areas are: (1) The Psychological World, (2) The Social World, (3) The Sexual Self, (4) The Family, and (5) The Ability to Cope. For the gay or lesbian adolescent, this framework is particularly helpful, in that it assumes that an adolescent may master one aspect of the world while failing to adjust in another. The intrinsic difficulties in adjustment become even more clear when homophobia becomes part of the mix.

The psychosocial world of the gay or lesbian adolescent is, indeed, a complex one. For example, the process of adolescence that burdens them is also overlaid with the developmental process of coming out (Cass, 1979). This dual struggle creates the chance of fragmentation in the gay or lesbian adolescent's psychological development. Furthermore, the notion of internalized homophobia also cannot be ignored, in that the child must address such core issues as guilt and shame. Malyon (1984) suggests that adolescents have three common adaptions to this dilemma: (a) repression of same-sex desires; (b) a developmental moratorium in which homosexual impulses are suppressed in favor of a heterosexual or asexual orientation; and (c) homosexual disclosure and the decision to mobilize same-sex desire.

These adaptions further illustrate the potential for psychological fragmentation that exists for the gay/lesbian adolescent. If adolescents are not able to overcome core issues of guilt and shame surrounding their identity, it can be assumed that an element of fearing social rejection is operating that would cause them to either repress or suppress their same-sex desires, particularly as a coping mechanism to avoid identification by their heterosexual peer group and family. On the other hand, adolescents who choose to disclose their gay or lesbian identity are confronted with the same social rejection from both heterosexual and homosexual environments.

These youth are often scapegoated, ridiculed and rejected by both their peer group and their families. The child's coping mechanism may be to run away in a search for role clarity. It is well documented that these youngsters then become further alienated, neglected and isolated in their quest to integrate this crucial developmental stage of life (Bidwell, 1988; Gonsiorek, 1988; Martin, 1982; Martin & Hetrick, Malyon, 1984; 1988; Mercier & Berger, 1989; Remafedi, 1988). Drug and alcohol use and increased sexual behavior, potentially deadly combinations, often become the primary coping mechanisms for these youngsters. There is also the potential for exploitation by adults from whom these young people seek guidance during this vulnerable time.

THE ADOLESCENT AT RISK FOR HIV INFECTION

The argument has been made that the developmental stage of adolescence and its inherent tasks, combined with psychosocial forces, place all adolescents at increased risk for HIV infection. It seems reasonable to infer that, because of social rejection and denial of opportunity in the environment for developing a positive, affirming gay or lesbian identity, gay and lesbian adolescents are at even greater risk for HIV infection. Two questions, then, emerge. First, what defines the adolescent "at high risk" for contracting HIV? Second, how does that definition, or particular set or characteristics, or identified clusters of risk factors, impact our practice methodology?

Researchers studying a population of incarcerated youth (1992), found that adolescents who are gay or lesbian are among those most at risk for HIV infection. It was further determined that certain characteristics define those adolescents at most risk for contracting HIV, including those who are gay and lesbian: youth who have had a lifetime number of sex partners of 25 or more; homeless youth; youth identified as Satan worshipers involved in sharing blood and blood rituals; injection drug users (IDUs) who use at least once a week; youth who have prostituted, or who have a history of engaging in survival sex; female adolescents who have been pregnant more than once; and teens of both genders who have had at least three documented STDs upon current admission. Also at significantly elevated risk are youth with a documented history of sexual abuse, as well as hemophiliacs and those youth with a history of blood transfusions.

These characteristics, combined with the arguments presented earlier, serve as a backdrop for the profiles of two adolescents, a gay male, and a lesbian, both infected with HIV.

CASE STUDIES

Alex

Alex is a seventeen-year-old caucasian gay male, who is infected with HIV. Alex came from an extremely dysfunctional family who physically, sexually and emotionally abused him throughout his formative childhood years. At the age of 11, Alex ran away from home, began to prostitute himself to men for food and shelter, and became chemically dependent. These behaviors that Alex engaged in to meet his survival needs are believed to be how he contracted HIV.

Alex was placed in a GLASS group home by the Department of Children's Services. At the time of admission, his health was declining, and his prognosis for succeeding in the group home was poor, due to the lengthy time he had been on the streets, his chemical dependency, and his own stated lack of commitment to change, or even to remain in the group home. At the time of admission, he had not been receiving any medical care or other interventions for his HIV status. The youth service provider community in Los Angeles is highly organized and efficiently coordinated, thus able to effectively collaborate in providing needed services. Therefore, it was possible to move Alex very quickly into the service provider network, to insure not only his aggressive medical treatment in order to slow the progress of the disease, but also his shelter and care during his numerous absences from the group home program.

There were several drug and alcohol relapses and runaways from the group home. During these episodes, Alex was housed by various shelters within the provider network. As a result, his whereabouts were generally known by his Children's Service worker and his GLASS social worker pretty quickly, so that there was no break in service provision. Eventually, intensive counseling and case management began to bring positive changes in Alex's life. He was enrolled in a special medical care program designed for adolescents, drug and alcohol treatment, and received intensive counseling that brought stability into his life for the first time. Although Alex's health continues to decline, the quality of his life has vastly improved. In large measure, it was due to the coordination of efforts among several agencies, that enabled effective service delivery to Alex.

Achieving stability in Alex's biopsychosocial situation was challenging in itself. However, as he became more receptive and compliant with psychosocial interventions, other developments occurred that illustrate the importance of multi-agency coordination of services *at all levels of intervention,* as well as the need for social policies that can move the bureaucracy. His medical condition made him eligible for SSI benefits. When Alex applied for these benefits, his application was approved, even though he was a minor at the time, without any kind of inquiry as to his living circumstances. As a result of receiving SSI benefits, Alex became partially ineligible for group home care. This policy essentially split Alex from the team trying to help him. Simply, Alex believed that his benefits should go to him to use as he pleased. For the group home, the reduction in reimbursement rate seriously affected the ability to meet his costs of care. Consequently, Alex attempted to emancipate with inadequate skills and resources. He was soon back on the streets, prostituting and consuming drugs and alcohol. Continued contact and psychosocial interventions resulted in Alex agreeing to readmit himself to the group home.

Shortly after Alex was readmitted to the group home, another policy issue emerged. His behavior on the street left him in poor physical health with a significant weight loss. Additional physical symptoms indicated that Alex might have been in the beginning stages of the wasting syndrome. His physician prescribed the dietary supplement, ENSURE, to assist Alex with weight gain. This product was not covered under Alex's state-sponsored health insurance, Medi-Cal. At a cost of $175.50 per month, it was difficult for the group home to pay for ENSURE, so the case manager sought other resources for the product. Several AIDS service organizations carried this product for their clients, free of charge. However, Alex was denied access to this product at one agency because he was a minor, and their services were available only to adults, and was refused at another agency because of his status as a resident of a group care facility, which they assumed was being reimbursed to provide for this commodity. This problem illustrates the need for further refinement of policy issues both among AIDS service agencies, and within the public sector (in this instance, Medi-Cal), to insure that youngsters with minor status, such as Alex, do not "fall between the cracks" of service provision eligibility.

Jennifer

Jennifer is an eighteen-year-old lesbian, who was infected with HIV at the age of 15, as the result of her only heterosexual sexual experience. During this same time period, Jennifer was abandoned by her mother after many years of intra-familial conflict, which resulted in her being placed in foster care. Soon after her foster home placement, her HIV status was discovered. Her foster parent refused to allow Jennifer to remain in care, and insisted that Jennifer be removed within hours of learning her HIV status. Jennifer was able to be admitted to a GLASS group home, and remained in residence for approximately two years. Because of her HIV status, it was felt that she would benefit more from being in a group home, rather than a GLASS foster home, since the level of services available to her would be much higher in a group home. Throughout her placement in GLASS, Jennifer was a model resident. She complied with all medical treatments and appointments, responded well to counseling, completed integration of her lesbian identity, and received As and Bs in school. As she neared emancipation, she worked with her case manager in locating her own apartment and enrolled at a local university to pursue studies in social work.

Jennifer candidly discussed her HIV infection with peers, staff and other professionals. She gave frequent interviews to the press, and appeared on numerous television shows, both locally and nationally, and soon became a media spokesperson for adolescents with HIV. This exposure prompted a national talk show host to donate a car to GLASS for Jennifer to use when she emancipated. Soon after this donation, Jennifer was asked if she would speak to a group of professionals about HIV. Jennifer's response was "not unless they pay me. I make too much money talking about HIV to do it for free."

The initial decision to allow Jennifer to appear in public settings was carefully thought out, and involved case management, social work, medical, psychological, and Children's Services input, as well as a consideration of Jennifer's wishes. Shortly after her emancipation from GLASS, despite ongoing case management support from GLASS's Intensive Case Management project, Jennifer dropped out of school, was evicted from her apartment because of loud parties, lost her job, and was unable to maintain the insurance on her car. Subsequently, Jennifer re-enrolled in school, resumed working, and was able to reinstate her auto insurance. In retrospect, Jennifer's maturity level was probably such that she was not able to handle the flurry of attention she received because of her HIV status, and the public exposure did not shore up her flagging self-esteem. Instead, it may have given her a false sense of importance, which evaporated when the media notice diminished.

These two cases illustrate both the unique contributing factors of HIV among gay and lesbian adolescents, and the profusion of barriers which impede practice strategies from meeting the service needs of these youngsters.

HIV REQUIRES A NEW PARADIGM

The social service professions have been caught off guard by the AIDS epidemic among gay and lesbian youth. What emerged was an illness for which there was no ready or easy cure, along with new and unanticipated social and psychological needs on the part of clients. Government was slow to address both the issue of HIV and AIDS and the population most affected by the disease, adult gay men. At the point that, as a result of pressure brought to bear by gay and lesbian activists, our political system began to address this as a serious social and potentially economic problem within our society, the approach remained reactive, incremental and remedial, and subjected to the slow and rigorous methodology of the medical model. Characteristics of this paradigm are that intervention is inexpensive, short-term, adapted for a slowly changing environment, based on a perceived weakness of the organization or the individual, problem oriented, and performance evaluated (Norman, 1992).

Norman claims that the entry point for a paradigm shift is for organizations addressing the problem of HIV and AIDS, or any other problem that emerges within an ever-changing environment, to revisit their stated purpose. Once it is determined that the purpose of an organization is remedial in nature, the mission and goals of the organization must be redefined for a new paradigm that is proactive and preventive. This requires that organizations anticipate change by adapting forecasting procedures, and by allowing for changes to occur in the culture of the organization. Characteristics of this paradigm include the concept that expense is not the issue; rather, the mission and goals are the issue. Thus, long range planning orientation prevails over management by crisis, and the organization becomes more responsive to a rapidly changing environment. Organizational actions deal with strengths and opportunities, and performance is compared to desirable behavior.

It is argued that the activism of the gay and HIV-infected communities has been the principle driving force for bringing about such a paradigm shift in the battle against AIDS. For example, as more and more of the gay community was being impacted by AIDS, a reaction occurred that "business as usual," or the old paradigm, ceased to be "good enough." A phenomenon occurred which galvanized the gay community, out of anger and the realistic fear they would once more be rejected and left to die, should the old approach be taken. Since there was no cure on the horizon and there was no palatable political response to the problem, a dramatic, proactive and preventive approach was developed within the gay and lesbian community. Organizations such as AIDS Project Los Angeles and the Gay Men's Health Crisis in New York, sprang up throughout the country. Their main mission was to provide for the biopsychosocial needs of those affected by HIV and AIDS. Extensive prevention efforts to educate people about safer sex were designed. Creative approaches were employed, such as bar campaigns, safer sex workshops, and media campaigns. In the absence of financial support from the government, massive sums of money were raised from within the gay community and from nongay supporters, to meet the rapidly growing psychosocial service needs of HIV infected persons.

The gay and lesbian community adopted a political action approach (Grosser & Mondros, 1985) in addressing the problem of HIV and AIDS, which contributed to the paradigm shift. Organizations such as ACT UP demanded that the medical and political systems address this problem in a proactive and urgent fashion, and reject outdated methodologies and approaches. ACT UP has been at the forefront, demanding increased funding for research, treatment, and prevention of HIV. Similarly, this organization has been a major proponent in advocating for change in existing medical research methodologies which are inherent within the old paradigm and wasting precious time in seeking a cure. ACT UP and other organizations have called for the government to authorize and fund a "Manhattan Project" approach to AIDS, one in which all possible resources would be mobilized until a vaccine and treatment are developed.

Finally, it is argued that the rapid emergence of HIV and AIDS, combined with the environmental forces described earlier, requires that social workers and others working in this area develop a more generalist, macro approach to practice with an emphasis in primary prevention that does not impede existing practice methodologies. This notion is supported in the literature. Germain (1984) argues that ecological ideas are reshaping social work practice, and are already observable. She further asserts that an ecological approach to social work practice provides a framework for developing primary prevention programs. For all adolescents, not only the gay or lesbian adolescent, this ecological approach seeking effective prevention strategies is essential, given that there is no cure for AIDS, nor does one appear on the horizon, and considering that adolescents' developmental life stage is laden with environmental hurdles that increase their risk for HIV infection.

To date, the literature supports the ecological approach to practice as it addresses the problem of HIV and AIDS among gay and lesbian adolescents. The primary emphasis is on the development and implementation of primary prevention programs that educate adolescents about HIV, and about methods of preventing HIV infection.

Hepworth and Shernoff (1989) argue that three levels of AIDS prevention should be occurring simultaneously in order to reach the many diverse segments of the population which includes adolescents. These levels are: (1) primary prevention which attempts to prevent the occurrence of any more new cases of HIV infection, (2) secondary prevention which is addressed to those who already have tested positive for HIV but are asymptomatic and, (3) tertiary prevention which is for persons diagnosed as having AIDS and focuses on reducing the disabling aspects of AIDS. For adolescents, the focus of AIDS prevention has been at the primary level (Flora & Thoresen, 1988; Hepworth & Shernoff, 1989; Kelly & St. Lawrence, 1988; Melton, 1988; Rotheram-Borus et al., 1991; Schwarcz & Rutherford, 1989).

Rotheram-Borus et al. (1991) argue that, while prevention efforts at the primary level have increased adolescents' knowledge of HIV and encouraged positive attitudes toward safe sex and drug related behavior, these interventions have not led to behavior change. She argues for more intensive primary prevention programs grounded in social learning theory. Specific features include:

> (a) a minimum of ten sessions, (b) assertiveness and coping skills training and acquisition of knowledge and positive attitudes toward safe sex, (c) identification of personal risk behaviors that are ranked in order of risk and systematically addressed and, (d) ongoing support for behavior change that is actively structured through group meetings for peer support and developing social norms for safe acts.

For adolescents, she calls for two additional components: (1) ongoing comprehensive care that also addresses youths' mental health needs and, (2) development of administrative protocols that anticipate crises, provide ongoing support for behavior change and establish an active, multilevel network of service providers.

The notion of providing comprehensive care was instituted by Health Start in its five school-based clinics in St. Paul, Minnesota (Naughton et al., 1991). This project provided assessment, counseling, education and referral for additional mental health services. In their sample of 626 adolescents, they found that levels of knowledge about HIV infection were high as were continuation of risk taking behavior in all areas except needle use. This study is limited in that it did not measure the impact of comprehensive care. Instead, the data collected were on participants' knowledge, behavior, and attitudes regarding HIV transmission.

The problems in Naughton's study illustrate only the surface of limitations in conducting sound research in AIDS prevention. These limitations are discussed by Kelly and St. Lawrence (1988), who argue that most prevention efforts in AIDS research have been conducted by community organizations with limited resources, focused on service provision rather than on research priorities. Compounding these limitations are methodological constraints, population access and sampling issues, ethical issues and, as Kelly and St. Lawrence (1988) state, "the urgency of a health crisis which compels the rapid implementation of applied prevention programs." Finally, Kelly and St. Lawrence (1988) argue that actual behavior change and risk reduction steps are influenced by factors other than increasing cognitive knowledge through educational interventions. The factors include:

the individual's ability to estimate accurately the level of risk associated with his or her behavior; expectations that behavior change efforts can be successfully undertaken; coping with antecedents that might otherwise trigger the health risk behavior; the presence of cues, reminders, and prompts to make and then to maintain risk-reducing changes; models that illustrate and sanction the desirability of behavior change, and ongoing environmental and social supports that encourage health-related behavior and discourage health-threatening behavior.

IMPLICATIONS FOR PRACTICE

The arguments presented earlier have numerous implications for practice with adolescents. First, the data are alarming. Adolescents, regardless of sexual orientation, are rapidly becoming one of the fastest growing populations at risk for contracting the HIV virus. This requires that everyone having contact with adolescents reexamine their values in their approach and interactions with this population. Competent practice requires a reexamination of one's homophobia, the manner in which that may impede practice, and the willingness to make professional behavior changes. Similarly, competent practice dictates that we actively engage our adolescent clients, their families, and the organizations where adolescents congregate (e.g., schools, religious youth groups, boy's and girl's clubs, etc.) to discuss the issue of sexuality, and provide a safe environment in which to explore an emerging gay or lesbian identity. It is essential that we normalize this stage of development.

The role of social workers as practitioners needs to be reevaluated in order to adopt a more generic approach to practice. For example, serving as a clinician may no longer mean functioning as a therapist. Instead, we may need to become educators, teaching adolescents about condoms, about safer sex, and distributing condoms. In addition, we must become advocates for change, training our peers about gay/lesbian adolescents and HIV, and demanding organizational and political policies designed to stop the neglect and discrimination on the part of mainstream agencies and society.

Our existing service delivery system also requires attention. For example, adolescents with HIV are uniquely different from their adult counterparts. The existing service delivery system has had years of dealing with adults, particularly adult gay men infected with HIV, and dying from AIDS. Governmental and organizational policies have been designed accordingly. Adolescents are not adults, and it is erroneous to believe they will fit into, or be able to maneuver within, a system designed for adults. This becomes apparent with those agency policies that exclude services and medication for HIV infected adolescents because of their age. It also becomes visible when child care licensing agencies will not alter their policies to accommodate these youngsters when no other service exists. Furthermore, adolescents are not developmentally or cognitively equipped to deal with these institutional, sociocultural, logistical, and financial barriers. The case management needs of adolescents are different from those of adults as well. Even the ability of an adolescent to obtain needed case management services is different. Because the difference is developmental, it is, therefore, not changeable by a particular intervention. Adolescents are not yet sufficiently psychologically developed in terms of even having enough self-esteem, or persistence, to press for needed services. They have not yet developed the skills needed to "work," or manipulate a system, in order to meet their needs. Finally, with so many different service delivery systems in place in both the public and private sectors, most adolescents are likely to feel overwhelmed by the sheer volume of paperwork necessary to access services, and will drop out. Thus, it will not be enough to simply allow adolescents adult case management systems. The systems must change to meet the needs of the adolescents.

It is also true that AIDS service providers are ill equipped to deal with the adolescent client. Many agencies refuse to provide service to the gay or lesbian adolescent, fearing that an accusation of recruitment will be lodged. Many simply do not want to provide service to a population that possesses such a complex set of problems.

CONCLUSION

Adolescents, especially gay and lesbian adolescents, have emerged as a significant subpopulation in the AIDS epidemic. In spite of this, our existing paradigm and approach to practice continue to ignore this fact. It is perplexing to note that an outmoded approach continues, despite significantly changing environmental and social conditions. These factors continue to serve as an oppressive agent, rather than a helping one. As a profession, we must reexamine our strategies in dealing with adolescents, sexuality, and HIV infection. It is important that we adopt a preventive, political action approach, before it becomes too costly for overburdened systems, and before the human cost is too high, and another generation is lost to this disease.

REFERENCES

Athey, J.L. (1991). HIV infection and homeless adolescents. *Child Welfare, 70*(5), 517-528.

Bidwell, R.J. (1988). The gay and lesbian teen: A case of denied adolescence. *Journal of Pediatric Health Care, 2*(1), 3-8.

Boyer, C.B. & Kegeles, S.M. (1991). AIDS risk and prevention among adolescents. *Social Science Medicine, 33*(1), 11-23.

Brownworth, V. (1992). America's worst-kept secret. *The Advocate, 599*, 38-46.

Cass, V.C. (1979). Homosexual identity formation: A theoretical model. *Journal of Homosexuality, 4*(3), 219-235.

Cochran, S.D. & Peplau, L. (1991). Sexual risk reduction behaviors among young heterosexual adults. *Social Science Medicine, 33*(1), 25-36.

Erickson, E. (1963). *Childhood and society.* New York: W. W. Norton and Co.

Feldman, D.A. (1989). Gay youth and AIDS. *Gay and Lesbian Youth* (pp. 185-193) New York: The Haworth Press, Inc.

Flora, J.A. & Thoresen, C.E. (1988). Reducing the risk of AIDS in adolescents. *American Psychologist, 43*(11), 965-970.

Germain, C. (1984). Social Work Practices in Healthcare: An Ecological View. New York: Free Press.

Goldstein, E.G. (1984). Ego Psychology and Social Work Practice. New York: The Free Press, 88-89.

Gonsiorek, J.C. (1988). Mental health issues of gay and lesbian adolescents. *Journal of Adolescent Health Care, 9*, 114-122.

Grosser, C.F. & Mondros, J. (1985). Pluralism and participation: The political approach. In Taylor, S.H. & Roberts, R.W., *Theory and Practice of Community Social Work* (pp. 154-178). New York: Columbia University Press.

Grossman, A.H. (1991). HIV and at-risk youth. *Parks and Recreation, 26*(11), 52-55.

Hepworth, J. & Shernoff, M. (1989). Strategies for AIDS education. *AIDS and Families* (pp. 39-80). New York: The Haworth Press, Inc.

Hingson, R.W., Strunin, L., Berlin, B.M., & Heeren, T. (1990). Beliefs about AIDS, use of alcohol and drugs, and unprotected sex among Massachusetts adolescents. *American Journal of Public Health, 80*(3), 295-299.

HIV & AIDS Quarterly Surveillance Report (September, 1993). The Centers for Disease Control, 1600 Clifton Rd., N.E., Atlanta, GA 30333.

Kelly, J.A. & St. Lawrence, J.S. (1988). *The AIDS Health Crisis: Psychological and Social Interventions.* New York: Plenum Press.

Los Angeles County Adolescent HIV Consortium. (1993). *The Los Angeles County Adolescent HIV/AIDS Strategic Plan: 1993-1996*, 1-43.

Malyon, A.K. (1981). The homosexual adolescent: developmental issues and social bias, *Child Welfare, 60*(5), 321-330.

Martin, A.D. (1982). Learning to hide: The socialization of the gay adolescent. In Feinstein, S.C., Looney, J.G., Schwartzberg, A.Z., & Sorosky, A.D., *Adolescent Psychiatry: Developmental and Clinical Studies* (pp. 52-65). Chicago: The University of Chicago Press.

Martin, A. D. & Hetrick, E.S. (1988). *The stigmatization of the gay and lesbian adolescent.* (pp. 163-183). New York: The Haworth Press, Inc.

Melton, G.B. (1988). Adolescents and prevention of AIDS. *Professional Psychology: Research and Practice, 19*(4), 403-408.

Mercier, L.R. & Berger, R.M. (1989). Social service needs of lesbian and gay adolescents: Telling it their way. *Adolescent Sexuality: New Challenges for Social Work* (pp. 75-95). New York: The Haworth Press, Inc.

Minton, H.L. & McDonald, G.J. (1984). Homosexual identity formation as a developmental process. *Bisexual and Homosexual Identities* (pp. 91-103). New York: The Haworth Press, Inc.

Morris, R., Baker, C., Huscroft, S. (1992). Incarcerated youth at risk for HIV infection. *Adolescents and AIDS: A Generation in Jeopardy.* Newbury Park, CA: Sage Publications.

Naughton, S.S., Edwards, L.E., & Reed, N. (1991). AIDS/HIV risk assessment and risk reduction counseling. *Journal of School Health, 61*(2), 443-445.

Needle, R.H., Leach, S., & Graham-Tomasi, Robin P. (1989). The Human Immu nodeficiency Virus (HIV) epidemic: Epidemiological implications for family professionals. *AIDS and Families* (pp. 13-37). New York: The Haworth Press, Inc.

Norman, A. (1992). Lecture Class, notes from, *Social Work 766.*

Offer, D. & Sabshin, M. (1984). *Normality and the life cycle: A critical integration.* (pps. 77-107, 364-425). New York: Basic Books.

Remafedi, G.J. (1988). Preventing the sexual transmission of AIDS during adolescence. *Journal of Adolescent Health Care, 9,* 139-143.

Rotheram-Borus, M.J., Koopman, C., & Ehrhardst, A.A. (1991). Homeless youths and HIV infection. *American Psychologist, 46*(11), 1188-1197.

Schwarcz, S.K. & Rutherford, G.W. (1989). Acquired Immunodeficiency Syndrome in infants, children, and adolescents. *Journal of Drug Issues, 19*(1), 75-92.

Slater, B.R. (1988). Essential Issues in working with lesbian and gay male youth. *Professional psychology: research and practice, 19*(2), 226-235.

Taylor-Brown, S. (1991). The impact of AIDS on foster care: A family-centered approach to services in the United States. *Child Welfare, 70*(2), 193-209.

Legal Challenges Facing
Lesbian and Gay Youth

Abby Abinati

SUMMARY. Legal constraints on minors can be especially problematic for lesbian and gay youth, who frequently lack support from their families and from school authorities, and whose circumstances are often misunderstood or disregarded by authorities throughout the juvenile system. Legal mechanisms exist or can be crafted to meet the needs of lesbian and gay youth who have been rejected by their families of origin. School, welfare, and juvenile justice administrators must become sensitive to the personal, economic, and societal pressures faced by lesbian and gay youth, and must tailor bureaucratic responses to the youth's particular needs. Finally, it is imperative that adults in the lesbian and gay communities take responsibility for protecting the interests of younger members of the community.

People who have not reached their 18th birthday are at a distinct legal disadvantage in our society. Their legal well-being is dependent in large part on the caprice of the adults to whom they are legally bound, primarily their parents, and secondarily the adults who direct the school, juvenile justice and mental health systems.

Abby Abinati received her Doctor of Jurisprudence degree from the University of New Mexico, School of Law. She is Legal Director and Director of Lesbians of Color Project for the National Center for Lesbian Rights, a San Francisco-based lesbian-feminist, multicultural legal resource center. Her tribal affiliation is Yurok.

[Haworth co-indexing entry note]: "Legal Challenges Facing Lesbian and Gay Youth." Abinati, Abby. Co-published simultaneously in *Journal of Gay & Lesbian Social Services* (The Haworth Press, Inc.) Vol. 1, No. 3/4, 1994, pp. 149-169; and: *Helping Gay and Lesbian Youth: New Policies, New Programs, New Practice* (ed: Teresa DeCrescenzo) The Haworth Press, Inc., 1994, pp. 149-169. Multiple copies of this article/chapter may be purchased from The Haworth Document Delivery Center [1-800-3-HAWORTH; 9:00 a.m. - 5:00 p.m. (EST)].

149

Lesbian and gay youth are more likely to be in relationship-shattering conflict with the adults in their world. Parents, educators, and health care providers often act out the bias of society against lesbians and gays. That bias, when combined with the uneven power of the relation of adults with minors, can result in brutalization of youth, as these adults enlist the force of the "law" to punish or coerce minor youth to conform to their ideal of heterosexual behavior.

Points of conflict include the parental relationship, the school environment, and the juvenile law system, which for purposes of this discussion, will include social services. There is some natural overlap among these areas, but separation here will aid clarity. In addition, the mental health care system can impact each of these areas, and the discussion of that system will be interwoven with each conflict point.

PARENTAL RELATIONSHIP

Guardianship

Very real schisms often erupt in families when a person in the process of awakening to her/his sexuality seeks to identify as lesbian, gay, or bisexual. This identification can be a precursor for rejection of these youth by their families of origin. The tenor of that rejection has serious consequences for these youth, who have been afforded inadequate safety nets by society. The well-being of youth is predicated on them being in a protective parental relationship with an adult or adults, preferably with their family of origin. If an adult(s) seeks to terminate the familial relationship by the act of banishment, what are the options of a person who has not reached her/his 18th birthday? The main legal options are seeking guardianship (or possibly adoption) or emancipation, and a possible civil suit for support combined with the options of guardianship and emancipation. The other options that exist are foster care, moving in with peers with sympathetic parents, or taking to the streets to eke out a survival existence.

Concentration on the statutory scheme of California in this discussion is meant to be representative of the schemes which are operative in most states, though this will not be absolutely true in all states. Since California is being used as a representative model, statutory cites will be to the California codes.

Guardianship in this context will refer only to those guardianships formed pursuant to the Probate Code;[1] those formed pursuant to the Welfare and Institutions Code will be discussed in the juvenile law section. According to the Probate Code, Section 1514, the court can appoint a guardian when it is "necessary and convenient." To appoint a non-parent guardian, the court must find (1) that custody with parent(s) would be detrimental to the minor (if a parent contests), and (2) that it would be in the "best interests" of the minor to live with the proposed guardian (Civil Code Section 4600).

This discussion will concentrate on guardianships of the person. However, if the youth has independent financial resources or the possibility of accumulating such resources, it may become necessary to consider a guardianship of the estate. Both of these guardianships can be done simultaneously, but the issues for guardianship of the estate are different and will not be discussed in this paper. There is precedent in juvenile law for youth to "divorce" their parent(s), i.e., to seek another adult(s) figure to assume the parental role or to seek the "shelter" of the child protective service. In theory, it would seem that youth could claim a right to be parented, and/or a right to support for their maintenance. Realizing that such a claim may result in a contested action, the strategy should be carefully considered to insure that the youth's primary goal of an alternate family is not jeopardized.

Lesbian and Gay Guardianships

In the instance of lesbian and gay youth, a great deal of animosity may exist between the youth and their parent(s). That animosity may take the form of a parent refusing to consent to a guardianship, or contesting on the basis of the parent's "right" to parent according to religious dictates or heterosexual models which reject any non-heterosexual lifestyle choice. Parents may also contest on the basis of the fitness of the proposed guardian(s), particularly if the youth has sought a lesbian or gay guardian(s). Youth advocates would be well advised to establish a bank of suitable prospective guardians for youth who find themselves in the position of being hostages of hostile families or of being banished. When considering guardianship, all parties must be aware of the responsibilities of the proposed relationship. In California, they include the duty for the care, custody, control, and education of the youth (Probate Code Section 2351); the right to determine the residence of the youth (Civil Code Section 2352); and, the right to give consent for medical treatment (Civil Code Section 2353). In certain limited cases, the guardian may be statutorily liable for civil damages resulting from a youth's willful misconduct, just as a birth parent might be. Although parents remain responsible for financial support, that obligation generally falls to the guardian. A youth may be eligible for receipt of public benefits. In such cases district attorneys will seek reimbursement from parents. Finally, the court must be advised of address changes and must give approval before the youth can be moved out of state.

When lesbian and gay youth are actively seeking a guardian, it is often an indication of the complete breakdown of their relationship with their parent(s). The court will often look to the desires of youth, in California giving particular deference to youth 14 and older–even allowing them to file a petition on their own behalf to name a guardian. Additionally, practicality requires that an older youth's adamant refusal to return to the family of origin must be given great weight by the court in considering whether to name the guardian agreed to by the youth.

Depending on the depth of the conflict, the familial relationship may have deteriorated to the point where actual abuse or neglect has occurred, creating an issue of the fitness of the parents. If these conditions exist, they will become considerations for the court in trying to address the court's real desire to have a familial structure for persons under 18 years old. Unfortunately, the necessity of raising these issues if the parents refuse to consent to the guardianship may well exacerbate the existing conflict in the family of origin.

Another issue to be aware of in preparing for a contested guardianship is whether the mental health of the youth will be called into question. Often times parents will have sought to "cure" their teenagers of their lesbian or gay sexual orientation. In so doing they will have created a mental health history of assessment, treatment or institutionalization for declaring their "deviant" sexual identity. If this has occurred, it will be essential to have the available records reviewed and to have the youth assessed by a responsible psychological expert who does not consider lesbian or gay sexual orientation to be an indicator of mental instability or illness.

In seeking a guardian, youth will often favor a home environment with a lesbian or gay guardian. The difficulty of establishing a guardianship in favor of a lesbian or gay guardian will depend on the state of the law in each jurisdiction. The first analysis is to determine if a state's statute directly prohibited the establishment of such a guardianship. If a state prohibits such a guardianship, then a decision must be made about the advisability of challenging that law through litigation. The second analysis is to determine if the state has a sodomy law, because it is likely that a non-consenting parent or a hostile court would raise such a law as a basis for disallowing the guardianship on the basis of unfitness.

The third and final analysis is to examine custody and adoption law in the state, in order to determine the trends in custody or adoption of youth by lesbian or gay parents. There are often unifying factors in these areas of law, e.g., the California best interest statute is used as a backdrop to custodial issues. Where that is true, some states, including California, have found that the legal status of being lesbian or gay is not per se prohibitive of custody. The courts require instead that a connection be made between sexuality and unfitness, and will not assume unfitness based solely on sexuality. Recognizing that courts may be reluctant to extend custodial rights to non-biological parents where sexuality is an issue, the issue may need to be balanced by the agreed advantages of a relationship between youth and specific parental figures.

Adoption

Adoption, although a legal option, would not generally be utilized because, unlike the guardianship situation, it is necessary to terminate the parental rights of the parents in the family of origin. This requires a much higher standard of proof, with a need to prove substantial abuse, neglect or abandonment. Also, the level of commitment is different: in a guardianship, the parties are forming a relationship which legally ends when the youth becomes 18. An adoption, by contrast, binds the new parent(s) financially and creates a lifetime commitment which excludes the youth's family of origin.[2]

Emancipation

Emancipation as used in this context is defined by statutory procedures established for the specific purpose of allowing youths to be freed from the custody and control of their parents before they are 18 (Civil Code section 62).[3] The goal of this procedure is to position the emancipated youth for treatment for many purposes as if the individual were 18 years old. There are negative aspects to this procedure from a community standpoint: Why should lesbian and gay youth be deprived of a supportive adult environment because their declared sexual orientation isolates them from their family of origin? Emancipation places the burden of meeting survival needs on the youth seeking to be emancipated.[4] There is a basic unfairness in shifting this significant burden to youth at a time when they are grappling with the difficulties of being teenagers coupled with the challenge of formulating an identity that has negative societal overtones. Serious thought should be given to the creation of model emancipation programs that create an extended family of choice for lesbian and gay youth who choose to become emancipated. Such programs would provide adult role models who would agree to take on the responsibility of an extended family in the ideal, i.e., supportive individuals to celebrate life with and to rely upon in the moments when crises or disappointments occur.

Pursuant to California's emancipation statute, Civil Code section 63, emancipated youths are treated as 18 for the following purposes:

a. They can consent to medical, dental, or psychiatric care without their parents' permission, knowledge, or liability for doctors' bills;[5]
b. They can enter into various kinds of financial transactions, such as: making a binding contract; buying, selling or leasing real or personal property; suing or being sued; settling a legal claim; and engaging in other kinds of transactions having to do with property and inheritance;

c. They give up the right to support from parents;
d. They gain the right to keep earnings from work (parents are legally entitled to the earnings of unemancipated minors), and to be free from parental control;
e. They gain the right to establish a residence of their own;
f. They are no longer under the jurisdiction of the juvenile court as court dependents (Welfare & Institutions Code section 300) or as status offenders (Welfare & Institutions Code section 601);
g. They can apply for a work permit (Education Code section 49110) without parental consent;
h. Their parents are no longer liable for damage caused by their wrongful actions (with certain exceptions);
i. They can enroll in school or college without parental consent.[6]

Youth are still treated as under 18 in several respects, for example:

a. They remain under the jurisdiction of the juvenile court in criminal prosecutions (Welfare & Institutions Code section 602);
b. They remain subject to restrictions on smoking, drinking, and working in places where alcohol is served (Penal Code section 308; Business & Professional Code sections 25658; 25661-25665);
c. They remain subject to labor laws barring them from certain dangerous types of work;
d. They cannot vote (United States Constitution, amend. XXVI, section 1);
e. They remain subject to age restrictions of driving (Vehicle Code sections 12507-12509); under the Vehicle Code section 17705, emancipated youth can get a driver's license without parental consent, if they have insurance;
f. They remain subject to compulsory school attendance laws;
g. They cannot give consent to sexual intercourse, so that a person who has sex with an emancipated minor is subject to prosecution for statutory rape.

For emancipation to be a viable legal alternative, youth also need the support of the lesbian and gay community, because the necessary prerequisites of stable housing, school attendance, and self support are tremendous obstacles to people ages 14-18 with no employment history. It requires the support of individuals and institutions to create these life support systems. Youth or their advocates seeking legal emancipation should work with the emancipation manual prepared by the Legal Services for Children, Inc. See note 6 herein.

EDUCATION

Lessons in Homophobia

High school, a difficult time for most people, is often a nightmare for lesbian and gay youth. Based on the most reliable figures available (Kinsey, 1948), it is reasonable to assume that the high school population is approximately 10 percent lesbian or gay.[7] High school is traditionally viewed as a supportive environment for students who are doing the hard work of developing their identities, often including their sexual orientation. It is also often the environment that socializes people as to community values.

Unfortunately, for lesbian and gay youth and for their heterosexual counterparts, what is often learned in high school is disapproval of lesbian and gay lifestyles. Homophobic school environments become the breeding ground for bigotry. A 1991 study of college age youth conducted by the American Council on Education and the UCLA Higher Education Research Institute found that 56% of the male students and 34.5% of the female students would prohibit homosexual relationships. That disapproval is encouraged in a hostile environment that gives both covert and overt approval to ridicule from teachers, uneven enforcement of disciplinary rules, verbal and physical assaults of lesbian and gay youth, and censorship of texts or library books that show tolerance toward lesbian or gay persons.[8]

Dropping Out

This harsh environment can be a strong causal link to the decision by many lesbian and gay youth to forfeit their education. Students faced with the twin hostilities of negative school environments and parents who disapprove of their emerging sexual identities face another potential brutality, i.e., the danger of being labeled a Special Education Child or Severely Emotionally Disturbed ("SED"). Youth who attempt to fight or resist the hostility of their home and school environment run the risk of being identified as rebellious. That can and has lead to these youth being placed in locked residential treatment facilities outside of California. (California does not allow its children to be locked or physically restrained in community based facilities, but other states have no such prohibitions. California's prohibition is not sufficient to protect our youth, as there are few regulations governing the interstate shipment of youth.)

This is a very real problem for lesbian and gay youth, as demonstrated by the story of Lyn Duff, a 16-year-old lesbian from South Pasadena who has chosen to go public with her story in an effort to stop the abuses of the SED programs. SED youth can be placed in these facilities without the benefit of a due process hearing, and without representation of the youth. Parents can send "problem" youth to these out-of-state locked facilities and then apply for funding, or apply for funding before commitment. The only proof involved is the requirement to demonstrate the "need" of the commitment. The hearing is an administrative hearing and concentrates on justification of the request for special status in terms of, is the school district liable for payment? There are no provisions to protect youth, no advocate who is there only for the youth. Ms. Duff was placed against her will in a secure Utah program by her mother in December of 1991. (This placement cost approximately $51,000.) She had "escaped" during home visits on two occasions, and in June of 1992, caught a bus to San Francisco.

At that point Lyn decided to "divorce" her mother. The case went to court and, in late 1992, two lesbians who have been partners for a decade became her permanent legal guardians. Today, she lives with her now "moms" and their young daughter in San Francisco. According to court papers filed on her behalf, clinical experts in San Francisco who examined Lyn saw no need for residential treatment. (Lyn's mother reportedly had her examined by four experts in Los Angeles before finding an expert who would say Lyn required "treatment.")

Legal Disputes in Public Schools

Legal issues involving lesbian and gay students in public schools fall into two categories of discrimination: claims regarding restrictions on freedom of speech and association, and claims involving due process rights.

1. Freedom of Speech

Freedom of speech is a guarantee of the first amendment of the United States Constitution. It protects what one says, what one writes and one's right to meet freely with other people in clubs, organizations, rallies and demonstrations. In California, there are two special laws which specifically protect students' right of freedom of speech and press at school. These laws give special guarantees against censorship of newspapers, yearbooks, handing out leaflets, wearing buttons, and posting notices on school bulletin boards.[9]

In spite of these guarantees, recent court rulings have held that school officials are entitled to control student expression "so long as their actions are reasonably related to legitimate pedagogical concerns."[10] What this means for the lesbian and gay student is still pretty much an open question. The only reported case directly involving lesbian and gay students in a high school setting is *Fricke v. Lynch*.[11] The court held that a male student's desire to bring a male date to the high school prom had "significant expressive conduct" and therefore was protected by the first amendment. The *Fricke* case extended free speech to social conduct that dealt with sexual orientation.

It is important to keep in mind that schools will offer various justifications for restricting first amendment rights. Schools will seek to justify the restrictions of first amendment rights by establishing that the form of communication is disruptive to school life and a danger to the welfare of other students. In *Bethel School District No. 403 v. Frazer*,[12] the Court gave school officials much greater discretion in controlling student expression. It upheld the suspension of a high school student who gave a sexually suggestive speech during a school assembly, noting that the speech provoked raucous behavior by some students and embarrassment in others, and concluding that "vulgar and offensive" language is inappropriate in public schools. In 1988 the Court affirmed the broad censorship powers of school officials, in *Hazelwood School District v. Kuhlmeier*.[13] It upheld the decision of a high school principal to delete from the school paper an article on student pregnancies and an article on divorce. The court held that school officials are entitled to control student expression.

2. Due Process

Due process rights are claims involving suspensions (long and short term), disciplinary transfers, exclusion from extracurricular activities and academic sanctions. All students have a right to be treated fairly: Any discipline imposed by a school official or variations in treatment of students must not be arbitrary. If a lesbian or gay student is threatened with school discipline or exclusion from a school activity because of her or his sexual orientation, a strong argument can be made that the school officials are acting arbitrarily in violation of those due process rights.

Consider the case of a student named Robert, from Ohio. Robert was a senior, a member of the All-State Chorus, Thespian and French Clubs, and was open about being gay. Robert wore a button on his jacket that said "I like men." He wore it for about a week without incident. The principal spotted the button and told Robert to remove it or he would be suspended. According to Robert, other students walked the halls with sexually explicit tee shirts and buttons but were not told to remove them. Robert was fortunate enough to be able to seek counsel, and when asked a few days later to remove the button, he responded that he had a right to wear it. The principal took him into her office with the intention of suspending him. Before the principal could say another word, Robert handed her his attorney's card and told her to call him. The principal decided not to suspend Robert after calling the district office, and Robert continues to display his button on his jacket.

3. Verbal Abuse

Lesbian and gay students are often subjected to name-calling by their peers, as well as by their teachers. It is not unusual for a lesbian or gay student to be refused protection when she/he asks for help in stopping threats and assaults by students.[14] Administrators too often ignore the pleas, reasoning that the lesbian or gay student has brought on the situation. One lesbian student described a class in which the teacher constantly spoke about the lesbian and gay population as a group that was not normal and not welcome in the community. Another gay student explained, "'straight' classmates are never punished for verbal or physical assaults on lesbian and gay students in my school." Such incidents are only some of the many ways in which lesbian and gay students are continually faced with having their rights violated because of their sexual orientation.

Administrators must ensure that the school climate is not oppressive. Schools should institute and enforce rules that protect lesbian and gay students from harassment, including verbal abuse. Schools can try to bring awareness of students' diversity to the forefront by developing anti-slur policies in cases of homophobia, just as they would in cases of racism.

The bottom line is that there are students in almost every classroom who are, or who will be, lesbian or gay. They need support and protection, and an opportunity to mature into sensitive, confident, productive adults, regardless of their sexual orientation.[15]

CHILD WELFARE AND JUVENILE COURT SYSTEMS

Before people reach the age of eighteen, if in discord with "supervising adult(s)/parent(s)," or if circumstances "force" them into a desperate survival decision (for instance, running away), they can become entangled with the juvenile court system. The court has jurisdiction over persons under the age of 18 who come within the provisions of Welfare and Institutions Code sections 300, 601, or 602:

> Section 300 pertains to minors who are abused, neglected, orphaned, abandoned, or are physically dangerous to the public because of a mental or physical deficiency, disorder, or abnormality. Section 601 pertains to minors who are alleged to be beyond the control of their parents, habitual truant, in violation of a curfew ordinance, or are runaways, but have not

committed a crime. Section 602 pertains to minors who violate any state or federal law or any city or county ordinance "defining crime," and covers violations of laws applicable only to minors, such as use or possession of alcohol. (Harris, Ed., California Juvenile Court Practice, Delinquent Minors, Vol.1)

Parental figures can become emotionally or physically abusive upon disclosure or discovery of a young person's actual or perceived sexual orientation. That abuse may result in the parent being referred to the juvenile system. In California, a parent can be reported to the police or to the county agency that contains the local branch of the child protective service. An investigation will follow. Initially, an evaluation will occur to determine if the parent(s)' actions are serious enough, e.g., harmful enough to result in a criminal complaint being filed against the parent. If a criminal complaint is filed, a parallel action in juvenile court will be filed to determine the placement of the young person. Even if no criminal action is filed, depending on the seriousness of the abuse, a juvenile court action will still be filed.

Juveniles faced with abusive actions by their parental figures can file a complaint, as can other family members or members of the public. Penal Code section 11165-11174 mandates that the following must report child abuse: "any child care custodian, health care practitioner, or employee of a child protective agency." Penal Code section 11166(a).[16]

A "child care custodian" is a teacher, administrative officer, supervisor of child welfare and attendance, or certified pupil personnel employee of any public or private school; administrator of a public or private day camp; licensed day care worker; administrator of a community care facility licensed to care for children; Headstart teacher; public assistance worker; employee of a child care institution, including, but not limited to, foster parents, group-home personnel and personnel of residential care facilities; social worker; or probation officer. Penal Code 11165.7 (a).[17]

A " health practitioner" is defined as a physician, surgeon, psychiatrist, psychologist, dentist, resident, intern, podiatrist, chiropractor, licensed nurse, or persons licensed under Division 2 of the

Business and Professions Code section 500-4979; dental assistant or hygienist, acupuncturist, midwife, clinical laboratory technician, speech pathologist, audiologist, optician, physical therapist or physical therapist assistant, vocational nurse, nurse practitioner, optometrist, hearing aid dispenser, osteopath, physicians' assistant, nursing home administrator, pharmacist, psychiatric technician, veterinarian, or animal health technician.[18]

"Child protective agency" is defined as a police or sheriff's department, a county probation department, or a county welfare department.

If a parent is reported to the juvenile system and a petition is filed, the juvenile court system will step in to work out a disposition with the family. If the petition is found to be true, the court has several options, depending on the severity of the abuse and the willingness of the parties to reconcile. Those options include having the youth return home under the supervision of the social services department; or, making an out-of-home placement, either in a foster or group home, or with a relative or friend of the family. (Note: Close relatives are spared the need to be licensed or certified foster homes; "friends" must have licensed or certified homes.)[19]

The goal of juvenile court actions in all but the most egregious cases is to reunite the family. For a period of no longer than eighteen months, the social service system will provide reunification services including family counselling. If the youth does not return home by the end of that period, reunification can still occur, but no services are given (or continued) to assist the family, and a permanent placement plan is made for the youth which is monitored by the social services department. Special services should be set up to work through the stress on the family of realizing that a member is lesbian or gay.

Court ordered family counseling which is sensitive to working through the societal bias against lesbians and gays should be a mandatory starting place. If it becomes clear that the youth will need a relatively permanent alternative placement, special care must be taken in seeking a placement. It is essential that the youth be placed in a lesbian or gay-affirming placement. For that reason, placements in group homes and county or state facilities should be carefully scrutinized to make sure that the youth will be protected.

In the $11 billion community care facility industry in the United States, programs specifically designed to meet the needs of lesbian and gay youth in placement are virtually non-existent.[20] These gay youth, like their adult counterparts, are vulnerable to physical and sexual abuse in society as a whole, and specifically in institutional settings. The courts and those working with youth must be sensitive to the precarious situations of young lesbians and gays, and guard against increasing the risks which may further endanger these youth.

An added dimension to this problem is that, if a youth is referred or self-referred into the system and becomes a "public charge" (i.e., receives public benefits, foster care benefits, etc.), then the parent(s) may become financially liable for the cost of the out-of-home placement. This may add to the strain of reconciliation if the family feels financially threatened, may become an incentive to reach an understanding, or may in an unfortunate scenario prompt a false reconciliation that leaves the youth with no support.

Young lesbian or gay people may fear the constraints of social service supervision, or be angry at a system that labels them as dependent youth and subjects them to the possibly equally hostile environment of out-of-home placement. Youth avoiding the "dependency" label may find themselves becoming "status offenders," i.e., only the status of their age makes their act a violation. Status offenders are considered beyond the control of their parents, are found in violation of a curfew ordinance, or are runaways who have committed no crimes.[21]

Status offenses are often a legally sanctioned blaming of the victim. Juvenile laws lurched into the 1990s supporting the myth of Ozzie and Harriet at home. They are based on the outdated notion that youth are running away to join the circus or to avoid having to do chores, so the misbehaving youth must be forced to return home. Running away is seen as just a part of growing up. With repeat or "serious" offenders, treatment or rehabilitation often concentrates on return of the youth to the environment from which she/he has fled, by concentrating on the behavior of the youth. It is essential that, at least in intake procedures, reform be initiated to find the root cause of a youthful status offender's reasons for desiring not to be at home, so that appropriate services can be devised. Prior to the

1980s when it became a widespread practice to ask during juvenile intake procedure about sexual abuse, many juvenile systems saw this type of "acting out" as indicative of youth in need of supervision, instead of youth attempting to survive. However, these systems found that youth would answer honestly to simple questions from intake workers; it was the intake workers' level of discomfort that had to be overcome. A similar discomfort exists with inquiries of sexual orientation. It is necessary to overcome that discomfort, so that intake at the status offender level can include specific questions to determine if a youth is in conflict with her/his family because of sexual orientation issues. Intake and psychosocial workup procedures and forms should incorporate the matter of sexual orientation into the process in a normalizing fashion, and avoid causing it to stigmatize the youth being evaluated.

Lesbian or gay youth who make the extreme decision to become runaways are often on the way to a precarious existence. They are forced by their age into the desperate position of trying to earn a living without any skills, with no legal way to circumvent the child labor laws, and with no access to public assistance unless they have a child. In all likelihood, they leave home with little or no money, and they are drawn very quickly into the whirlpool of poverty and homelessness.[22]

Lesbian and gay youth face harsh options. They need money in order to survive, so they begin to work in the areas of commerce most open to them: prostitution, the drug trade or other illegal activities.[23] When this happens, the youth are in line to become "delinquent minors," the term for youthful "criminals." Society forces these youth to take desperate measures, and then gives them criminal status under Welfare and Institutions Code section 602. If the juvenile system is to make any sense rather than being a mirror of the criminal adult system, if it is to offer youth a disposition that is cognizant of their needs, then the intake system must be sensitized to the issues of lesbian and gay youth. Probation officers, defense attorneys, and courts must not only concentrate on the crime, and rehabilitation, punishment, or restitution for the criminal act, but also must examine the circumstances which force youth to make impossible choices. If the juvenile system feels compelled to affect only the criminalized behavior of the youth who are in the system, then lesbian and gay youth will be at further disadvantage. They will be socialized in a system that is increasingly acknowledged to be unsuccessful in rehabilitation or deterrence, and will be exposed to peers whose choices may not have been substantially motivated by survival requirements.

All people respond to socialization. Lesbian and gay youth who have no anchor because their families have abandoned them are necessarily susceptible to those who offer survival solutions, even though those solutions may be high risk.

The options offered to lesbian and gay youth are so limited, that criminalized behavior is often the only life-affirming choice for them. To incarcerate these youth is fundamentally unfair. Whether for rehabilitation or punishment, incarceration places young lesbians and gays at risk of physical abuse from their peers. Additionally, these youth are faced with stigmatization as criminals through a system that offers no real answers to their dilemma.

Just as it is essential to identify at the intake level whether a youthful offender is a lesbian or gay youth in a survival mode, it is equally essential that the dispositional phase be cognizant of this factor. Dispositional alternatives must be reviewed with the risk factor to the youth considered, and the alternatives must be specially constructed to address the survival needs of the lesbian or gay youth. In addition, the disposition must address the alienation of youth who have been forced into criminal or commodity behavior by society's dislike of who they are. When people are forced to bargain with their bodies as economic units, society must expect and address the resultant emotional harm that is likely to spring from that experience.

These youth, like the section 300 youth discussed earlier (juvenile court dependent as a result of abuse, neglect, or abandonment), need the support of a lesbian and gay-sensitive environment. If they do not receive that support, they are at risk of paying an inordinate price for their sexual orientation. Placements must be developed which understand the stress that youth encounter from establishing their minority sexual identity status, and from the resulting lack of options. These placements must have a life skills component, and must to a certain extent rely upon the lesbian and gay community to provide not only role models, but also actual jobs and/or placements to allow youth to reach goals of emancipation or guardianship.

CONCLUSION

Lesbian and gay youth must not continue to be the last item on the agenda of the lesbian/gay civil rights movement. We in the movement must begin to see ourselves as part of a culture, and as such, we must choose between the models of individualism or group identity and responsibility. In this paper, I have argued for the model of the group, seeing the movement as an extended family. As adults, many of us have felt alienation from our families of origin and created our families of choice. Until the recent decades those families have not included the young, but I would argue that those youth kicked out of their families of origin are as much "ours" as any birth or adopted child. Further, if we wish them to claim us as we age, we must model family responsibility for them or accept that their alienation will mirror our own as we become senior citizens. Parental relationships should be based on care given. We have not been model parents to this point, but we should individually and collectively consider our responsibilities to lesbian and gay youth. Abandoning them to the juvenile system is cruel, and our movement will be diminished if we do not assume our rightful leadership role in seeking viable options for these youth.[24]

NOTES

1. The author is indebted to the *Guardianship Manual: A Guide To Obtaining Legal Guardianships (With Specific Examples From San Francisco County)*, prepared by: Legal Services for Children, Inc., 1254 Market Street, Third Floor, San Francisco, CA 94102, (415) 863-3792, for the legal substance of this discussion.

2. Although it is the exception, third parent adoptions have been granted in California. The underlying premise of these adoptions is that the law should recognize construct familial relationships. It is conceivable that a family of origin might consent to an adoption that allowed for them to maintain their parental rights while allowing the youth to live with her/his family of choice.

3. Youths may become emancipated by getting married (parents and court must give permission), joining the armed services (parents' permission and con-

sent of the service required), or being declared emancipated by a judge, under the procedure set out in Civil Code section 64.

4. Youths seeking to emancipate pursuant to Civil Code section 64 must prove in court that they meet the following requirements: they are at least 14 years old; they are willing to live separate and apart from their parents with the consent or acquiescence of their parents; they manage their own finances; they have a source of income, which does not come from any illegal activity; and emancipation would not be contrary to their best interests.

5. Some medical services including contraception, treatment for venereal disease, pregnancy-related treatment and treatment of alcohol and drug addiction are available in California to unemancipated youths without parental consent or notice. See Civil Code section 34.5, 34.7, 34.10.

6. The author is indebted for the substantive legal discussion to the *Emancipation Manual: A Guide To Obtaining A Legal Emancipation in California (With Specific Information for Alameda, Contra Costa, Marin, Napa, Santa Clara, San Francisco, San Mateo, Solano and Sonoma Counties)*, prepared by Legal Services for Children, Inc., 1254 Market Street, Third Floor, San Francisco, CA 94102, (415) 863-3792.

7. The Kinsey Institute for Sex Research reports that 9.13 percent of the United States population have had either extensive or more than incidental homosexual experiences. See Kinsey et al. (1948). *Sexual Behavior in the Human Male*. Philadelphia: Saunders.

8. See, *Gay Youth and the Right to Education*, Yale Law and Policy Review, Vol. 4:446, 1986.

9. These laws are found in Calif. Educ Code section 48907 and 48950.

10. See *Hazelwood School District v. Kuhlmeier*, 108 S.Ct 562, 572, (1988) and more recently *Poling v. Murphy*, 872 F2d 757 (6th cir 1989).

11. 491 F.Supp 38 (D.R.I.1980)

12. 478 U.S. 675, 678 (1986)

13. 108 S.Ct 562, 570 (1988)

14. Forty-five percent of gay males and 20% of lesbian females experience verbal or physical assaults in high school. Twenty-eight percent of these youth are forced to drop out of school because of harassment resulting from their sexual orientation. Source: National Gay & Lesbian Task Force (1984), "Anti-Gay/Lesbian Victimization." New York.

15. NEA Affording Equal Opportunity to Gay and Lesbian Students Through Teaching and Counseling: A Training Handbook for Educators.

16. A "commercial film and photographic print processor" is required to make a child abuse report when photographic materials depict a child under the age of 14 years engaged in an act of sexual conduct. Penal Code section 11166(c).

17. In addition, Welfare and Institutions Code section 307.5, provides that employees of a community service program who receive minors taken into protective custody are "child care custodians."

18. Child abuse must also be reported by a medical examiner or any person who performs autopsies if discovered during an autopsy, whether or not the abuse contributed to the death.

19. The juvenile court has the ability, independent from the probate court guardianship discussed above, to establish a juvenile court guardianship. This guardianship can be ordered at the end of the reunification process or earlier if the offense of the parents is serious enough to terminate reunification or if the parent(s) agree. Some courts will allow the guardian to continue to receive public funding. The home placement standards for a guardianship are less stringent than for foster care placement.

20. Gay and Lesbian Adolescent Social Services (GLASS), a Los Angeles-based agency operates the only group home programs *specifically licensed* to serve lesbian and gay minors. GLASS also certifies and supervises lesbian and gay-affirming foster homes.

21. Welfare and Institutions Code section 601 (b) pertains to misconduct at school, including truancy, whether the cause of the "misconduct" is mistreatment at school. Youths who flee misconduct should not be labeled the offender; instead like the predominately young women who are tired of being sexually harassed by male peers in school and may have avoided school, they should be assisted in their efforts to have a harassment free educational experience.

22. In an interview with the Larkin Street Youth Center in San Francisco, the Center reported contact with about 2000 homeless teenagers, about half of whom are lesbian or gay.

23. Up to half of the gay/bisexual males forced out of their homes engage in prostitution to support themselves, greatly increasing the risk of HIV infection. Source: Savin-Williams, RC (1988), "Theoretical Perspectives Accounting for Adolescent Homosexuality," *J. Adolescent Health Care*, 9(2)95-104.

24. Thank you to Rachel Bernstein, attorney at law, for editorial assistance; to Bernice "Berns" Portervint, law clerk for research and drafting assistance, particularly in the education section; and to law clerks Meeta Gawande, Kimberly Da-Silva, and Leslie Thrope for their helpful editorial comments.

REFERENCES

Gibson, P. (1989). Gay male and lesbian youth suicide. In U. S. Department of Health Human Services' *Report of the secretary's task force on youth suicide, 3*, 110-142.

Hazelwood School District v. Kuhlmeier. (1988). 108 S.Ct. 562.

Kinsey, A., Pomerey, W., & Martin, C. (1948). *Sexual behavior in the human male*. Philadelphia: Saunders.

Legal Services for Children, Inc. (1990). *The guardianship manual: A guide to obtaining legal guardianships*. San Francisco.

Legal Services for Children, Inc. (1990). *Emancipation manual: A guide to obtaining a legal emancipation in California*. San Francisco.

National Education Association (1988). *Affording equal opportunity to gay and lesbian students through teaching and counseling: A training handbook for educators.* New York: Basic Books.

National Gay & Lesbian Task Force. (1984). Anti-gay/lesbian victimization (pamphlet). New York.

Poling v. Murphy (1989, 6th Circuit) 872 F.2d.757.

Savin-Williams, R.C. (1988). "Theoretical perspectives accounting for adolescent homosexuality." *Journal of Adolescent Health Care, 9*(2), 95-104.

Yale Law and Policy Review (1986). "Gay youth and the right to education." Vol. 4, p. 446.

Index

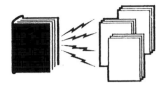

Haworth
DOCUMENT DELIVERY
SERVICE
and Local Photocopying Royalty Payment Form

This new service provides (a) a single-article order form for any article from a Haworth journal and (b) a convenient royalty payment form for local photocopying (not applicable to photocopies intended for resale).

- *Time Saving:* No running around from library to library to find a specific article.
- *Cost Effective:* All costs are kept down to a minimum.
- *Fast Delivery:* Choose from several options, including same-day FAX.
- *No Copyright Hassles:* You will be supplied by the original publisher.
- *Easy Payment:* Choose from several easy payment methods.

Open Accounts Welcome for . . .
- Library Interlibrary Loan Departments
- Library Network/Consortia Wishing to Provide Single-Article Services
- Indexing/Abstracting Services with Single Article Provision Services
- Document Provision Brokers and Freelance Information Service Providers

MAIL or *FAX* THIS ENTIRE ORDER FORM TO:

Attn: **Marianne Arnold**
Haworth Document Delivery Service
The Haworth Press, Inc.
10 Alice Street
Binghamton, NY 13904-1580

or **FAX:** (607) 722-1424
or **CALL:** 1-800-3-HAWORTH
(1-800-342-9678; 9am-5pm EST)

PLEASE SEND ME PHOTOCOPIES OF THE FOLLOWING SINGLE ARTICLES:
1) Journal Title: _____

    Vol/Issue/Year: _____ Starting & Ending Pages: _____

Article Title: _____

---

2) Journal Title: _____

    Vol/Issue/Year: _____ Starting & Ending Pages: _____

Article Title: _____

---

3) Journal Title: _____

    Vol/Issue/Year: _____ Starting & Ending Pages: _____

Article Title: _____

---

4) Journal Title: _____

    Vol/Issue/Year: _____ Starting & Ending Pages: _____

Article Title: _____

(See other side for Costs and Payment Information)

COSTS: Please figure your cost to order quality copies of an article.

1. Set-up charge per article: $8.00
   ($8.00 × number of separate articles) _____

2. Photocopying charge for each article:
   1-10 pages: $1.00 _____
   11-19 pages: $3.00 _____
   20-29 pages: $5.00 _____
   30+ pages: $2.00/10 pages _____

3. Flexicover (optional): $2.00/article _____

4. Postage & Handling: US: $1.00 for the first article/
   $.50 each additional article _____
   Federal Express: $25.00 _____
   Outside US: $2.00 for first article/
   $.50 each additional article _____

5. Same-day FAX service: $.35 per page _____

6. Local Photocopying Royalty Payment: should you wish to copy the article yourself. Not intended for photocopies made for resale. $1.50 per article per copy
(i.e. 10 articles x $1.50 each = $15.00) _____

GRAND TOTAL: _____

METHOD OF PAYMENT: (please check one)

❑ Check enclosed ❑ Please ship and bill. PO # _____
(sorry we can ship and bill to bookstores only! All others must pre-pay)

❑ Charge to my credit card: ❑ Visa; ❑ MasterCard; ❑ American Express;

Account Number: _____ Expiration date: _____

Signature: *X*_____ Name: _____

Institution: _____ Address: _____

City: _____ State: _____ Zip: _____

Phone Number: _____ FAX Number: _____

MAIL or *FAX* THIS ENTIRE ORDER FORM TO:

Attn: **Marianne Arnold**
Haworth Document Delivery Service
The Haworth Press, Inc.
10 Alice Street
Binghamton, NY 13904-1580

or FAX: (607) 722-1424
or CALL: 1-800-3-HAWORTH
(1-800-342-9678; 9am-5pm EST)